GW00359912

the Idler

ISSUE 40 | WINTER 2007

1 2 5 7 9 10 8 6 4 2

Published in 2007 by Ebury Press, an imprint of Ebury Publishing

A Random House Group Company

The Random House Group Limited Reg. No. 954009

Addresses for companies within the Random House Group can be found at
www.randomhouse.co.uk

A CIP catalogue record for this book is available from the British Library

The Random House Group Limited makes every effort to ensure that
the papers used in our books are made from trees that have been
legally sourced from well-managed and credibly certified
forests. Our paper procurement policy can be
found on www.randomhouse.co.uk

Typeset by Christian Brett

Cover image by Damien Hirst

Printed and bound by Firmengruppe APPL,
aprinta druck, Wemding, Germany

ISBN 978-0-091-92300-6

Editor Tom Hodgkinson
Deputy Editor Dan Kieran   *Creative Director Emeritus* Gavin Pretor-Pinney
Editor at Large Matthew De Abaitua   *Literary Editor* Tony White   *Sports Editor* John Moore
Music Editor Will Hodgkinson   *Motoring Editor* Fanny Johnstone
Special thanks to Chloë King & Jason Beard

To buy books by your favourite authors and register for offers visit www.rbooks.co.uk

WHAT IS ? THE IDLER

The Idler is a magazine that celebrates freedom,
fun and the fine art of doing nothing.

We believe that idleness is unjustly criticized
in modern society when it is, in fact,
a vital component of a happy life.

We want to comfort and inspire you
with uplifting philosophy, satire and reflection,
as well as giving practical information to help
in the quest for the idle life.

the Idler

CONTENTS

ISSUE 40 ❖ CARNAL KNOWLEDGE ❖ WINTER 2007

CONVERSATIONS

ESSAYS

STORIES

IDLE PURSUITS

EDITOR'S LETTER

WELCOME TO ISSUE 40 OF THE IDLER. YOU'LL NOTICE a change to the look of the magazine. Typesetter Christian Brett of Bracketpress has set the articles in Eric Gill typefaces for a classic, crafted feel which we also hope is beautiful and easy to read. We are also placing ourselves in a radical tradition of carefully set and printed pamphlets and magazines. We hope you like our new direction.

❖

This is the Sex issue and we've collected our favourite writers and artists to contribute their reflections on this perennially fascinating topic. Michael Bywater argues that we need to divest sex of its modern franticism and put the languor back in. Sex should be about ease and sensuality, not performance and hard work. Nicholas Lezard wonders what happened to all the fun and Neil Boorman wonders whether everyone else really is getting more than him. In conversation, therapist Esther Perel argues that we need to bring playfulness and wildness into the domestic sphere. We've got wonderful work from Gee Vaucher and Penny Rimbaud, and Jay Griffiths writes on the Lords of Misrule and the true spirit of Christmas, with illustrations by Alice Smith. Our cover by Damien Hirst expresses the life and humour that should be wrapped up with sex.

Elsewhere Kevin Godley of 10cc fame talks to Paul Hamilton about drugs, creativity, the tyranny of cool and the smoking ban, and we offer tips for the idle life in our Idle Pursuits section.

So take the day off, get a bottle of wine and sit under a tree all day with your beloved.

Tom Hodgkinson

At

INCLINE PRESS

we make books that are worth keeping.

They are hand made using archival quality materials, printed with metal type and 19th-century machinery. We only work on books that interest us personally, and we have broad interests, especially around 20th-century arts, crafts, and popular culture.

Each book we publish is a deliberately designed craft object, as thoughfully made as a hand-turned bowl or a hand-woven rug. Just as a weaver must choose yarns, colourways, and pattern before beginning to weave, so we select the typefaces, the illustrations, the cloth and paper for book and binding, all of which is intended to complement the text that has first engaged us. And so, by virtue of its bibliosity, each book becomes more than the simple sum of its parts — with all the work done by hand, publishing for us is a process rather than an event. Complex books take time to complete, and we usually publish four or five books each year. Every book gets a printed prospectus, and we put details on our web site.

If you would like your address to be put on
the mailing list, please contact us.

Graham Moss & Kathy Whalen INCLINE PRESS
36 Bow Street, Oldham OL1 1SJ, Lancs., England
Phone 0161 627 1966   www.inclinepress.com
books.inclinepress@virgin.net

CONTRIBUTORS

MATTHEW DE ABAITUA's debut novel, *The Red Men*, is published by Snowbooks

NEIL BOORMAN's book *Bonfire of the Brands* is published by Canongate

DAVID BRAMWELL needs to be punished

TOM BEARD is a twenty-year-old photographer. www.myspace.com/tombeardphotography

CHRISTIAN BRETT runs Bracketpress at www.bracketpress.co.uk

JAMES BRIDLE is a struggling polymath. www.shorttermmemoryloss.com

LINDSAY BRUNNOCK used to work in film and TV before becoming an illustrator

JAN BUCQUOY is a Belgian anarchist, filmmaker, agitator and writer

GRAHAM BURNETT is a gardener and writer. www.spiralseed.co.uk

MICHAEL BYWATER is the author of the brilliant *Big Babies* (Granta)

GEMMA CAIRNEY is a stylist based in London. See www.gemmacairney.co.uk

WARWICK CAIRNS' book on measuring is out soon

BRIAN DEAN runs the Anxiety Culture website www.anxietyculture.com

BILL DRUMMOND's latest doings can be inspected at www.penkiln-burn.com

MARK FARLEY writes the 'Bookseller to the Stars' blog

RYAN GILBEY is a film critic

JAY GRIFFITHS *is the author of* Wild: An Elemental Journey (Hamish Hamilton)

PAUL HAMILTON's book of Peter Cook stories is published by Snowbooks

DAMIEN HIRST is an artist

TONY HUSBAND is a cartoonist working for *Private Eye* and others

SARAH JANES is having a baby

DAN KIERAN's latest book *I Fought The Law* is published by Transworld

NICHOLAS LEZARD really has nearly finished his book about fun

MARK MANNING is a writer, artist and musician. See www.zodiacmindwarp.com

KEVIN PARR is an angler and a gentleman

DANIEL PEMBERTON is a musician, writer and wiseguy

PENNY RIMBAUD has disengaged. See www.onoffyesno.com

JOCK SCOT is having a baby

ALICE SMITH is an artist. www.alice-wonderland.net

ROBERT TWIGGER has a new book out called *Lost Oasis*; more at www.extremerambler.com

GEE VAUCHER

GWYN VAUGHAN ROBERTS is a chronicler of the dark side

GED WELLS runs Insane and edits *Trisickle* skateboard magazine

TONY WHITE is the *Idler's* literary editor and author of *Foxy-T* (Faber and Faber)

CHRIS YATES is a fisherman whose latest book *How To Fish* is published by Hamish Hamilton

WILLIAM YATES is a young illustrator and mad musician

NOTES from the COUCH

IDLER'S DIARY

Despatches from the loafer's world

Anarchy in the EC

¶ I took a trip to the beautiful city of Antwerp in Belgium to
promote *How To Be Free*. There I went out for dinner and many drinks
with Corinne Meier, author of the great *Bonjours Paresse*, and Jan
Bucquoy, the renowned Belgian anarchist. This sex mad free spirit
performs a *coup d'état* every year, attacking the Belgian palace in
Brussels. He runs his own bar in the capital, which has had
support lately in the unlikely form of the culture minister, who is a
situationist and fan of Guy Debord. Strange country. Antwerp itself
is very laid back and reasonably-priced. There are lots of cobbles
and old churches. The beer is superb, as are the chips. We talked
about sex, suicide and American cars. It's a paradise. Everyone
should move to Belgium and help Jan dismantle the State apparatus.
His new book is called *La Vie Est Belge* and we are planning to
translate it as one of the first projects for the newly created Idler
Books. 'Paradise, right here, right now!' is the subtitle of the work
and any French readers can get a copy from Michalon, and English
readers can sample it in this very magazine (see pages 29–30). TH

Still Smokin'

¶ There's been only one man brave enough to fight the government
on the insane smoking ban, one man with the balls to mount an
attack against this infringement on a British liberty as sacred as the
tea break. Not only that, this gallant warrior has had the cheek to
engage the services of Cherie Blair to fight his corner. Step forward
that noble, pink-suited libertine, Dave West Esq, owner of Hey Jo
and Puss In Boots, two London lapdancing clubs. Mr West made his
fortune with *Eastenders*, the Calais fags and booze chain. Now he is
defending the right of his punters to smoke in his clubs. 'I regard

my premises as an extension of my home and do not see why
people should be stopped from smoking,' he told the *Daily Mail* in
June. 'It is an invasion of their human rights. The only way for
patrons to smoke after July 1 is by going out on the pavement and
that could land me in trouble with the police if it creates noise or
disturbance. I am calling on other nighclubs to join me in the
challenge.' Good luck to you Mr West. The *Idler* is glad to lend its
support to your campaign.

Turn off Your Mind, Relax and Float Downstream

¶ In June earlier this year three brave adventurers set off from
Lowestoft (the most easterly point in England) on a journey to
Lands End (furthest west) on a 1958 milkfloat to prove the merits
of slow travel and green transport. Our intrepid trio, Dan Kieran,
Ian Vince and Prasanth, knew they would have to rely on the kind-
ness of strangers to charge their float, christened 'The Mighty One'
after Che Guevera's motorbike, because it can only manage thirty
miles with full batteries that take six hours to charge, but even they
were taken aback by the electric generosity they met on the road.
Their epic journey, driving over six hundred miles at a top speed of
just fifteen miles per hour, led them to some strange places but if
they made it to Lands End the cost of fuel (electricity) for their

entire trip would be a mere £12. They ended up charging up in a
bed factory, a Morrisons' car park, a luxury five star hotel, a
Benedictine monastery, loads of pubs (including a haunted one),
caravan sites and numerous kitchens across the country. On route
they discovered enlightenment, super noodles and a country seemingly most at ease with itself when helping total strangers complete
on a bizarre quest.

¶ To find out if they made it look out for the book and Radio 4
programme, called *Three Men In A Float* in May 2008. DK

The Good Life Here and Now

¶ There's only one think tank worth thinking about and that's the
New Economics Foundation, who customarily print their name in
lower case, I guess in an ee cummings-style gesture of humility.
Look out for their new book, *Do Good Lives Have To Cost The Earth*, a
compilation of essays on good living with a contribution from
yours truly. It's published by Constable and Robinson. The very idea
of a think tank is a nice one: somehow these guys have managed to
arrange things so that they are paid to ponder and reflect. And their
policy director, Andrew Simms, has written a terrific attack on
Tesco's called *Tescopoly*, highly recommended. Furthermore, another
associate, one David Boyle, telephoned me to talk about fairies and
troubadours. What style, what panache! TH

Street Life

To Soho, for tea with the laconic, witty and brilliant journalist Barbara Ehrenreich, who ealier this year published *Dancing in the Streets: A History of Collective Joy*, with its marvellous cover picture of dancing peasants by the great Flemish painter Bruegel. Ehrenreich will be known to many readers for her attacks on the US work culture, *Nickel and Dimed* and *Bait and Switch*. In *Dancing in the Streets*, a more academic book, she writes of the urgent need to reconnect with our festive spirit, and indeed blames an epidemic of depression and general misery on the lack of merriment in our lives. That evening she gave a live interview at a packed ICA, conducted by Geoff Dyer, who had just returned from the Burning Man festival in Nevada. The audience told Geoff that he didn't need to travel to the US to enjoy himself, and we agreed on the need for more free local festivals. A great talk and a great book, and we hope that Ehrenreich will contribute to future issues of the *Idler*. 🐌

If you have a diary story for us, send it to: mail@idler.co.uk.
£25 for each one published.

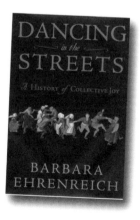

READERS' LETTERS

Send us your thoughts and reflections and tell us what you're up to.
Our address is: The Idler, PO Box 280, Barnstaple EX31 4WX

GOD AND LOAFING

Dear Idler

The atheist lives freely without dread of an afterlife, but the price he pays is a suspension of scientific reasoning. He observes matter and life, but without proof of an alternative he rejects outright one hypothesis as to their origin. The string theory of matter may propose dimensions and universes outside our own, but none of these could hold the creator of the matter and life we know.

The problem of course is organised religion. Religions — run by men — say they represent God, and the atheist is painted into a corner from which he cannot challenge this claim.

But is there any reason why a personal God could not approve the atheist's view of organised religion, and prefer us to follow our hearts instead of a set of rules: even to be idle when we want to be? After all, good human parents are happy when they see their children enjoying themselves.

Peter Smith

LAND, LIBERTY AND THE GUILDS

Dear Idler

Some months ago I managed to blag a few quid from the Arts Council in order to create the 'Art-O-Matic'. This is a machine that displays a continuous loop of back-lit A2 posters; its compact size means that it can be used as a portable visual arts exhibition. Each time the exhibition is staged we invite people to submit new artwork for the next series of posters, we also provide practical training using up-cycled computers and open source software to encourage people to get creative. The event is inspired by Erich Fromm's teaching that 'we're creatures evolved to become creators' and the belief that suppressing our creative urges has led to the present epidemic of stress, depression and neurosis. As part of the project, I managed to collect a series of essays from a broad range of interesting and influential people who very kindly gave me permission to use their work.

One of those essays was 'Charters of Liberty in Black Face and White Face: race, slavery and the commons', written by the historian Peter Linebaugh (www.metamute.org/en/html2pdf/vie w/417). It provides some interesting information regarding the Magna Carta and the fact that we're usually only given half the story. The accompanying contract, 'The Charter of the Forest', seems to have been swept under the carpet. This is hardly surprising because whereas the Magna Carta seeks to ensure equality in *principle*, the Charter of the Forest demands equality in *practice*. Just as Magna Carta demands provides a basis for human rights by ensuring the basic principles of justice such as *habeas corpus*, trial by jury and prohibition of torture (each threatened by recent changes in legislation brought about by the supposed 'war on terror'), the Charter of the Forest sought to guarantee the good people of Albion the right to live off the fat of the land. According to the Charter of the Forest, each of us has the right to use the land for food, shelter, clothing, travel and fuel. This 'commons vs corporate' theme has inspired a completely new project that may be of interest to you.

Lincoln is a lovely town famed for its cathedral. It is also home to one of the few surviving copies of the Magna Carta. The document is on display in its own building in the grounds of Lincoln Castle. The display itself is looking a little lovelorn and could do with a bit of revamp, so with this in mind, I suggested to Peter Linebaugh that there should be a campaign to reunite the charters of liberty. He agreed, but was a little cautious. Living in a pit town I was politicised by the miners' strike and subsequently became involved with squatting, free parties, anti-poll tax, Earth First!, Reclaim the Streets etc. I wouldn't think twice about turning up at Lincoln Castle with a sound system, 200 crusties and a giant copy of the Charter of the Forest written in multi-coloured crayon, but I get the feeling that Mr Linebaugh would like things done a little more soberly.

So I'd like to enlist your readers' help in a campaign. I feel that if we can raise funds for the Lincoln Castle display whilst raising the profile of the Charter of the Forest then we'd also help to raise awareness of 'the commons' in general. The commons were essential to the Guilds system and woud be necessary to ensure the success of a new Federation of Guilds. The charters of liberty also provide a good foundation for a commons-based law of the land and can be an inspiration for future federal contracts.

Yours in anarchy, mirth and hope
Warrem Draper
warrendraper@supanet.com

SKIVERS & STRIVERS
Heroes and Villains of the Idle Universe

Skivers

Midwives

Doctors don't like them. Midwives are an anomaly in the over-medicalised process of birth and quietly cheer you on if you refuse to undergo labour wired up like a recharging fat android. We love them for relying on wisdom born of education and experience rather than the arbitrary dictates of a bureaucratic system, and thank them for bringing us a nice cup of tea after we popped out the latest sprog.

Hair gel

If you gave a million typewriters to a million monkeys, and then took those typewriters away and gave the million monkeys hair gel to play with instead, the laws of probability dictate that they would quickly come up with superior hairstyles to the passengers of the last train from London to Eastbourne.

The Meaning Of Life

Solved. Consciousness matters because it is its function to matter. The soul is the adaptive illusion of evolution, designing a self that feels it is so great it is worth preserving. That's it. We can all go home now.

Removal men

In the past, the stereotypical image of the removal man was a man in a tan overall dropping the family china or struggling with a piano up the stairs. The modern removal team, girdled by lumber support belts and loaded on Lucozade, barrel in and out of your gaff like it is an Olympic sport — however, for all their athleticism, they are still high on the ageless promise of zipping through the job and knocking off early. For smoking roll-ups while squinting at the long sofa and the narrow staircase, we salute you!

New underground magazines

From the 'seriously snazzy-fangled' New Rave rag *Super Super* to the quarterly of personal storytelling *Bad Idea*, it's good to see that even in this age of internet exhibitionism, hardy souls are willing to drive their sanity to the wall by publishing their own magazine. We're here for you if you ever need a cup of tea and a chat about salespeople who promise the earth but struggle to sell a single half-page black and white ad.

Sebastian Horsley
Splendid dandy who has spent a lifetime avoiding work and instead indulges in pleasure, art and living. His memoirs, *Dandy In The Underworld*, have just been published by Sceptre and we recommend the book highly: aphoristic, wise, funny and full of spirit.

❖

Strivers

Desks
Pupil, undergraduate, office worker — a life spent at the desk. And then comes death, and the final stately progress to the grave sealed in a desk with the lid nailed shut.

Songs Of Praise
Now onto its forty-sixth anniversary of ruining Sunday for children. Surely its time for the atheist's alternative: 'Songs Of The Void'.

Ethical AND stylish
I will only buy your ethical product if it makes me look good.
I will only give a fuck if you make me look cool.
Excuse me, isn't that the opposite of ethics?

360 degree appraisals
Apparently, this is not when you twirl around so that your line manager can admire your new gown. It is a modish performance measurement in the workplace, in which the employee or manager is subject to feedback from everyone their work touches. It is called 360 degrees because your head will turn a single revolution at the prospect of undergoing it.

That organic health food place
If you are so concerned about health, why is there a wall of Green and Black's chocolate in your shop? Even if the cocoa beans were grown up the arse of a Nicaraguan peasant boy, eating it will still make you fat and die.

Giving a Powerpoint presentation
'And on this graph I have plotted the rapid decline of my dreams upon the axis of the remorseless march of the years.' 🐌

Idle Pleasures

THE DECK-CHAIR

¶ Who does not love a deck-chair? Wittgenstein did. It was the only
item of furniture he allowed in his study at Trinity, Cambridge;
supposedly a testament to his asceticism, I instead saw it as the ideal
solution to the problem of how to manoeuvre something comfy to
sit on up the narrow stairs to my study. ¶ But that the greatest
philosopher of the twentieth century saw in the deck chair a
sufficiency of design and purpose — and Wittgenstein was no mean
designer himself — should say something about the perfect utility
of this furniture item. ¶ Firstly, they are absurdly simple. This might
strike anyone who has spent some time trying to figure one out as
counter-intuitive, to say the least. Indeed, the cruellest thing I have
ever done was watch a French *au pair* trying to erect a deck chair in
my garden without trying to help her — and it was one of those
deck-chairs with arms, which have a trick to them. But she had
been a bit snooty earlier, and I thought it was proper to remind her
that there were some things in which the Brits still had an edge.
¶ Master the art of deck-chair origami and you will wonder how
you ever managed without one. Imagine this: a chair so comfy you
can sleep in it which can be carried when not in use. The deck-
chair symbolises ad hoc leisure, snatched naps, impromptu basking.
The deck-chairs on Brighton pier are free for public use, unlike
many of those elsewhere; is there any finer way to spend a sunny
day, nursing a mild hangover, a packet of chips warm in one's lap,
while watching the parade of hedonists about one, or the continuous drama of the English Channel unfold itself before you?
¶ They speak to us of the sea, wherever they are; in my study,
relaxing in it, I hear the faint calling of gulls, and even, in deeper
reverie, the vanished days of the ocean liners whence they got their
name. Somewhere, a bell rings; it is time to rise, and dress for
dinner at the Captain's table. 🐚

Nicholas Lezard

Ged Wells

THE SOCIAL SCRUTINY GUIDE TO UK PERIL

A Department of Social Scrutiny Infoganda Leaflet
Channelled by Ian Vince / www.socialscrutiny.org

Since July 1, failure to accept that you are in constant mortal danger of one sort or another has become illegal inside public buildings in England and Wales.

As part of its remit to elevate natural unease about the world into full delusional paranoia, the Department of Social Scrutiny presents this handy guide to the National Peril Level Alert System. Not only will you find the degree of gut-wrenching panic appropriate at each level, but you will also discover what we can do to help you if you have a panic-impairment, a sceptical disposition or are in receipt of a related benefit, such as Incredulity Allowance.

Interim measures are available to help the chronically calm become more publically-spirited through fear. Specially designed outdoor shelters will be erected for those who persist in remaining placid, despite the mounting evidence against their anti-social habit, but to help those of a tranquil disposition to come to terms with the associated health risks, a random number of these shelters will be blown up by the government without warning.

ALERT LEVELS

The Banana Level Peril Alert indicates that it may be dangerous to be beyond earshot of a Police Constable, Community Support Officer or similar crime-fighting operative with a level of authority equivalent to or greater than 2 (two) ASDA store detectives.

If you find yourself beyond earshot of the appropriate person(s) of authority, you may experience a higher than recommended level of exhilaration and/or excitement for a short period. Counselling will be made available to all those with registered neuroses, but only where they do not stem from failure to adopt the consensus view on the IKEA shopping experience.

The government's robust attitude towards the Combined Forces of Evil hasn't all been a bed of roses and we have inevitably upset many, many madmen with weapons along the way. **The Merganser Level Alert** recognises they would now like to kill you in ways too painful to explain at length in this short pamphlet. Good luck with that. When a 'Merganser' is announced, you should fasten all the doors and windows of your property in the interests of energy conservation, but also so that your neighbours cannot hear you scream, "We're all going to die, we're all going to die".

Dealing with the Counter-Counter Insurgency

Naturally, the War on Terror will generate its own counter measures – we expect these to eventually lead to a War on War on Terror – and, indeed, the Department has already made contingency plans in order to plan for this contingency.

1. The exact position of London will be concealed, road signs and atlases will be altered to show the capital in the area currently occupied by Birmingham. The Pearly Kings will be evacuated to Dudley and instructed to talk loudly about the Queen Mother as a decoy. A massive infrastructure will be put in place to ensure a steady stream of jellied eels and new media start-ups.

2. Martial Law will be introduced and you must always obey the instructions of police officers, even if they appear far younger or less intelligent than you.

3. All UK TV will be suspended except E4, which will concentrate on Soviet era martial music punctuated by a single episode of Friends: *The One Where They Board Up All the Windows and Hide Under the Stairs.*

London ◉

The Snowy Owl Level Peril Alert communicates a level of niggling doubt about the medium to near-term future. When the level is at Snowy Owl, it is indicative of a higher level of worry than the anxiety generated over whether a gas hob has been left on during a two week Mediterranean holiday, yet lower than the prospect of a visit from a devoutly religious member of your extended family.

Emergency Numbers

Make a note here of any emergency numbers you may need during the emergency, in the event of another emergency.

The Lead Shielded Pizza Delivery Co . . . .

The 24-Hour Radiation Forecast Line . . . .

International Rescue: Thunderbird 2 . . . .

IAN VINCE

GOOD JOB:
FILM CRITICS

*Ryan Gilbey introduces our new series written
by people who enjoy what they do*

¶ When I get asked what I do for a living, it always seems the
done thing to temper my answer with some manufactured caveat
or wrinkle. Something along the lines of: 'Yes, I get paid to write
about films, but you should see what I have to sit through.' I usually
mention the Pokémon series, or anything starring Meg Ryan, to drive
the point home. It doesn't do to gloat. The truth is I can't think of
anything bad about my job. Sometimes the complimentary sand-
wiches at preview screenings are a bit rum: man cannot live by
egg mayonnaise alone. But even that's easily solved. You just bring
your own.

¶ I've been sitting in the dark now for over three decades, on and
off, though I've been paid to do it for less than half that time.
Over the years, occasional excursions into the outside world have
been unavoidable. But as far as possible I have remained loyal to
my cinema seat. You can't miss it: it's the one in the front row—
the spot traditionally favoured by Surrealists, intellectuals and the
short-sighted — surrounded by food wrappers and coffee cups.
I'm happy here. Why wouldn't I be? I've always loved cinema. Not
just the films themselves, but the ritual of entering this darkened,
subterranean world where you can abscond from real life for hours
at a time. I've never liked that feeling of being monitored that
comes with office life, and this job is more or less exempt from
that. If I'm reviewing a three-hour movie, it's going to take three
hours to watch. There's no arguing with that, no possibility of
stepping things up a bit. There is a looseness in my working life
that insulates the very pleasures which got me hooked on movies
in the first place.

¶ My Italian grandmother took me to matinées before I was old enough for school. We bonded over films. I would nudge her awake when she dozed off in the cinema. On the bus home, I always babbled about what we'd seen. She gave me movies, and taught me that it was healthy, even essential, to spend entire afternoons in cloudcuckooland.

¶ It wasn't an auspicious start — the first thing she took me to was a film of the sitcom *Man About the House*, which should by rights have functioned as aversion therapy. But I fell in love with the naughtiness of going to the cinema: all that pleasure and emotional stimulation, all that food, in the darkness, in daytime, while everyone else was at work. As I got older, I found ways to preserve that naughtiness. In my early teens, I wasn't allowed to go to the cinema on my own, so naturally I started going to the cinema on my own — to trashy films in run-down parts of town, and later to all-night movie marathons. College and university lectures struggled to compete with the lure of the matinée. The basic frisson of cinema-going for me still comes from being freed from normal life and responsibilities. Skiving off, I suppose you'd call it. Even when I'm working hard, it still feels like skiving off.

¶ Crucial to this sensation is the time of day. Cinemas are lively, sociable meeting places in the evening, when we are given license to spend our leisure time, our pocket money. That's no good. I prefer them in the mornings and afternoons, when they retain their furtiveness, their suggestion of secret or unorthodox pleasures. After seeing a film I like to mull it over for a day or so, turning it around in my head, examining it from different angles. To the casual observer, it might look like I'm napping or slobbing out or wandering through the park in a daze, but in here, in my head, I'm working. Honest. ◉

LIFE IS ABOUT CHEMICAL AND PHYSICAL EVENTS HAPPENING!
I SHIT YOU NOT!
BEING IN HERE IS DOING MY FUCKING HEAD IN!
LATER...
THE CUNT'S DEAD!

WORK
SERIOUSLY DAMAGES
YOUR HEALTH

In this extract from his new book, the Belgian anarchist Jan Bucquoy imagines what society will look like after his coup

¶ And work? Disgruntled people will say: we'll have to work hard, after the *coup d'etat*. I am not convinced … Today, concentration camps are called factories, offices, whereas two hours a day should be enough to put chips on your plate. Certainly, we'll forget about growth, which does nothing more than fatten up the shareholders who don't actually do anything. The only people who will be obliged to do mind-numbing work will be the crooks. That will be their only punishment, as the prisons will be knocked down.

¶ This will be a world upside down, which really means it will finally be the right way up. There will be no petty thieves, because we'll be living in a society of abundance and there will be no point in stealing phones, tellies or cars because we will get our fill from the lottery [goods such as these will be handed out by a lottery system]. As for drugs, there will be none either: Belgium itself will be like a shot of heroin, every five minutes. Crooks will no longer be the same as before: now they will be property owners who won't part with their houses, jealous husbands, bailiffs, trade unionists, heads of human resources … there will be an attack on ugliness: for work is ugliness. Makers of door keys and the developers of the Belgian coast who have changed it into a Monaco in the North must finally be called to account.

¶ The inhabitants of the liberated Belgium will benefit from a national basic income. They will be free to do what they want with it, after all, there are those people who are incurable and for whom the daily grind is a real drug. Work is the opium of the people. Every job offer and every pay slip will bear the following legend: work seriously damages the health. Yes, work makes us unhappy. It kills. It renders us powerless. The worker, the little employee, on his return home after a boring day, what does he do? He crashes out in front of the telly in order to forget? And the following morning, he takes pills and tablets in order to have the strength to get up and go to work for peanuts, for a salary which doesn't even allow him to get the beers in. Me, I propose the following:

1) The right to profit from one's morning erection will be enshrined in the Constitution. What makes people ill is that they don't fuck enough and they get bored too much. After the *coup d'état*, Little Red Riding Hood will have the right to knock down her grandmother and cock a snook at the wolf.

2) The only medicine allowed will be aspirin (a good antibiotic and excellent hangover cure), Viagra and Pill B [Bucquoy's heroin-and-arsenic suicide pill]. All other medicines are useless, all they do is soothe people who are not ill but unhappy: it's not the same thing. Me, I can tell you that unorthodox Belgians are never ill, and I know what I'm talking about. I enjoy a constitution (among other things) of iron becasue I don't work and I don't have health insurance. ◉

Extracted from Jan Bucquoy's book *La Vie Est Belge*, published by Michalon

THE TRUTH: CRIME

Brian Dean of *Anxiety Culture* says our fear of crime
is out of proportion with the reality

¶ The government is falsely lumping together crime, antisocial behaviour and
terrorism, to create the illusion of one big rising threat. Ministers apparently
intend to frighten the population into sacrificing basic freedoms for the sake
of 'security'.

SCARY CRIME HEADLINES

¶ The media has, for years, reported 'spiralling' crime. But the *British Crime
Survey* (regarded as authoritative by most criminologists) says the risk of
becoming a victim of crime is at "an historic low". Domestic burglary and
vehicle crime, for example, have more than halved over the past decade.
¶ Some sections of the media have focused on "rises" in violent crime.
The BBC, for instance, has provided the following headlines:

> "Violent crime figures rise by 12%" (22/7/04)
> "Gun crime figures show fresh rise" (21/10/04)
> "Violent crime increases by 6%" (25/1/05)
> "Violent offences top million mark" (21/7/05)
> "Violent crime and robbery on rise" (26/1/06)

¶ In fact, violent crime has fallen since 1995 — the official figures are clear on
this (an in-depth investigation by BBC's *Panorama* acknowledged the drop in
violence). The above headlines are misleading as they don't take into account
changes in recording practices (in 1998 and 2002) which have artificially
inflated violent crime figures. For example:

- Certain 'antisocial' behaviours (eg minor scuffles) have been
  reclassified as crime, with the effect of doubling recorded
  violent crime.

- A violent crime with several victims is no longer recorded as a
  single crime. An incident with three victims, for instance, is now
  recorded as three crimes.

¶ The artificial nature of the 'increase' in violence is confirmed by the Home Office's statisticians, who say that "recorded violent crime has been inflated over the last few years by changes in recording practices [...], increased reporting by the public and increased police activity." (Home Office Bulletin, July 2006).

BBC ADMITS ERROR

¶ On the *Ten O'Clock News* (BBC1, 20/10/05), Fiona Bruce announced that violent crime had "significantly" increased. I complained to the BBC that this was incorrect (the official figures showed that the "increase" — of 6% — was not "significant", but was an artificial inflation). The BBC's *Editorial Complaints Unit* eventually wrote back, after an investigation, and agreed that BBC1 news had breached editorial guidelines on "truth and accuracy", and that there was "no basis" for claiming a significant rise in violent crime. Moral: don't assume the BBC bothers to research its own news.

THE MYTHICAL GOLDEN AGE

¶ Decades of headlines on "soaring" violence give the impression that society is forever becoming more dangerous. This reinforces the conservative belief that we're undergoing a moral decline from some earlier Platonic Golden Age.

¶ Historic researchers present a totally different picture. Ted Robert Gurr, in *Historical Trends in Violent Crimes*, writes that, in Britain, 'the incidence of homicide has fallen by a factor of at least ten to one since the thirteenth century'. He adds that the 'long-term declining trend' in such violence is a 'manifestation of cultural change in Western society'. In other words, we're becoming more civilised over time.

¶ Manuel Eisner, in *Long-Term Historical Trends in Violent Crime*, claims that 'serious interpersonal violence decreased remarkably in Europe between the mid-sixteenth and the early twentieth centuries'. The urban historian Eric Monkkonen concurs: 'Personal violence – homicide – has declined in Western Europe from the high levels of the Middle Ages. Homicide rates fell in the early modern era and dropped even further in the nineteenth and twentieth centuries.'

ANTISOCIAL BEHAVIOUR

¶ Another alleged symptom of moral decline is "yobbish" behaviour. The government portrays this as a new and growing menace. Whitehall press officers were no doubt pleased with a recent ICM poll, for the BBC, which found that "lack of respect" topped the list of reasons why people felt Britain was "worse than 20 years ago". Crime and terrorism came second and third.
¶ Perhaps if we lived longer we'd have a sense of déjà vu over this. For example, in 1898, newspapers in England warned of the menace of 'hooligans' and of a 'dramatic increase in disorderly behaviour'. The Times reported ' organised terrorism in the streets'. In every decade of the 20th century there were similar media panics.
¶ One can go back even further in time and witness the same sense of alarm at a perceived moral breakdown:

- 'What is happening to our young people? They disrespect their elders, they disobey their parents. They ignore the law. They riot in the streets inflamed with wild notions. Their morals are decaying. What is to become of them?'
  (Plato, 4th Century BC)

- 'When I was young, we were taught to be discreet and respectful of elders, but the present youth are exceedingly disrespectful and impatient of restraint'.
  (Hesiod, 8th century BC)

- 'We live in a decaying age. Young people no longer respect their parents. They are rude and impatient. They frequently inhabit taverns and have no self control'.
  (Inscription, 6,000 year-old Egyptian tomb)

- In April 1738, the press covered a report from a British Government committee which had been set up to 'examine the causes of the present notorious immorality and profaneness'.

- In the 1800s, hordes of teens and pre-teens ran wild in American city streets, dodging authorities, 'gnawing away at the foundations of society', as one commentator put it. In 1850, New York City recorded more than 200 gang wars fought largely by adolescent boys.

• 'Juvenile delinquency has increased at an alarming rate and is eating at the heart of America'. (US juvenile court judge, 1946)

TONY BLAIR'S GRANDMOTHER

¶ Tony Blair's PR crusade against antisocial youth backfired recently. During a photo-opportunity, he hosed down graffiti and commented that older generations of his family would have abhorred such behaviour. The *Daily Mirror* then reported that Blair's grandmother was a 'commie' graffiti vandal.
¶ Blair also talked of a Golden Age when 'people behaved more respectfully to one another', but a friend of his late grandmother, Alex Morrison, 86, said: 'he is speaking absolute rubbish. Poverty and misery were widespread and it was a violent place as well'.

FEAR OF TERROR

¶ The police have often acknowledged that fear of crime is out of proportion to the risk of crime for most people in this country. The same is no doubt true of terrorism. According to the MIPT terrorism knowledge base, the total number of US and UK (including Northern Ireland) fatalities caused by terrorism in the five years after 9/11 was 74, compared to 68 in the five years before. The corresponding totals for Iraq are 15,763 and 12, respectively. That should put fear of terrorism into perspective for UK and US citizens.
¶ Unfortunately, as Michael Bond reports in *New Scientist*, people base their fears more on the vividness of events than on the probability of them reoccurring. And since television presents very vivid coverage of any attack (or foiled attack, rumoured attack, etc) on UK or US soil, it is 'destroying our probabilistic mapping of the world', according to Nicholas Taleb, professor in the sciences of uncertainty at the University of Massachusetts.
¶ There have been several terror scares in Britain since 2001. The Centre for Policy Studies published a report (*The Use and Abuse of Terror — The construction of a false narrative on the domestic terror threat*) which investigated a few of these, and found that despite media panic, they turned out to be nothing. The report's authors concluded (on Channel 4's *Dispatches*): 'We have shown that you can't believe a word that you read in the newspapers about the terrorist threat. We have also shown that the politicians are only too ready to use terror as a political tool.'

SCRAPPING MAGNA CARTA

¶ Winston Churchill said we must never stop proclaiming 'the great principles of freedom ... Magna Carta, the Bill of Rights, the Habeas Corpus, trial by jury...'. All of these, in theory, place limits on state power.

¶ Tony Blair, however, has argued for a "complete change of thinking" in our legal system — he wants to remove what he sees as outdated constraints in tackling new threats. Echoing Blair, the head of MI5 says 'the world has changed and there needs to be a debate on whether some erosion of [civil liberties] may be necessary to improve the chances of our citizens not being blown apart'.

¶ These arguments imply that crazed outlaws now pose a greater danger to society than our legal system has ever had to deal with. But this is contradicted by historic and contemporary evidence for each type of threat, so our alarmist leaders conflate several dangers — crime, antisocial behaviour, terrorism, identity fraud, etc — into one big apocalyptic nightmare.

¶ Then, taking this phoney doom-scenario as a premise, they conclude the world has changed as never before, requiring that we sacrifice our freedoms for 'security'. It's an exercise in circular reasoning that would have us pay billions in tax to fund mechanisms removing fundamental liberties. ⊚

(Sources, respectively: Home Office Statistical Bulletin [HOSB], containing British Crime Survey, July 2003 & July 2006; BBC Online coverage of quarterly crime figures, 2004–2006; HOSB, July 2006; Panorama BBC1, 17/4/05; Guardian, 22/4/05; HOSB, July 2006; HOSB, October 2005; Gurr, Historical Trends in Violent Crimes, 1981; Eisner, Long-Term Historical Trends in Violent Crime, 2003; Monkkonen, Homicide: Explaining America's Exceptionalism, 2006; ICM poll, BBC Online, 4/9/06; Battered Britain, Channel 4 booklet, 1995; Egyptian inscription quoted in Buckminster Fuller's 'I Seem to be a Verb'; Fortean Times no. 39; Barry Glassner, The Culture of Fear, p75–76; Daily Mirror, 16/1/06; MIPT figures, tkb.org; New Scientist, 19/8/06; Centre for Policy Studies/Dispatches, C4, 20/2/06; Churchill speech, 5/3/1946; Blair speech, Labour Party conference, 2005; Eliza Manningham-Buller [MI5] speech, 1/9/05)

The Wit and Wisdom of
MAE WEST

Paul Hamilton salutes the pleasure-loving revolutionary in diamonds

¶ Mae West, the sassy lass of Brooklyn, was an outrageous self-invention. Already forty by the time of her film debut (*Night After Night* in 1932), she had been a Broadway star during the previous decade with her self-penned plays celebrating the pleasure principle. Incurring the wrath of uptight moralists and other cross-making bores — the title of one show, *Sex*, was enough to get them fulminating and frothing with apoplexy — West was a one-woman army against prudery and hypocrisy, who turned her own shortcomings (podgy face, slothful gait) into attributes. She was a revolutionary in diamonds rather than khaki. In an age where women were meant to be obscene but not heard, she was outspoken in her desires. A sexual table-turner, Mae dominated her helpless suitors. Women wanted to be her and men wanted to be in her. An irrepressible flirt, in a courtroom scene she slowly (of course) sashays past the jury that are meant to be judging her, purrs 'How'm I doin'?' and takes them all in with eyes that might be auditioning them for a private orgy. It is she who judges them.

¶ In the age of James Cagney and Clark Gable, fast-talking go-getters, Mae went to the opposite extreme. She would drawl her lines and never be more than languorous to the point of somnambulance in her movements. Even lines of dialogue that had no obvious sexual *double-entendre* would be left hanging in the air, just in case ...

¶ After only a couple of films into her screen career, the League Of Decency joined forces with Hollywood's Motion Picture Production Code in an attempt to crack down on lewdness, suggestiveness and loose morality. Mae suffered badly. There was no room for an independent woman living a life of material and sexual satisfaction on her own terms when there was the Great Depression hanging over the States. She capitulated in *Klondike Annie*, where she played a tart-with-a-heart who joins a Christian mission to save souls with the Good Book (UGH!). Subsequent films found her invariably robbed of her true voice — she was no longer the creator of her own scripts.

¶ The following selection of West witticisms are, it's pertinent to recall, as much as eighty years old. Consider what mindbombs these casually-delivered bon mots were back then and how familiar some of them are. Like the joyous human spirit they sprang from, they remain delicious and indestructible.

I wasn't always rich. There was a time I didn't know
where my next husband was coming from.

❖

When women go wrong, men go right after them.

❖

Cary Grant: Have you ever found a man that's made you happy?
Mae: Sure … Lots of times.

❖

Maid: I thought you were a one-man woman.
Mae: I am. One man at a time.

❖

Maid: I don't see how any man can help loving you.
Mae: I don't give 'em any help. They can do it themselves.

❖

When I'm good I'm very, very good — when I'm bad I'm better.

❖

Cary Grant: I don't know if I can trust you.
Mae: Of course you can. Hundreds have.

❖

It's not the men in your life that counts, it's the life in your men.

❖

Hat-check girl: Goodness, what lovely diamonds!
Mae: Goodness had nothing to do with it, dearie.

I'm the kind of gal who works for Paramount all day
and Fox all night.

❖

Suitor: Aren't you forgetting you're married?
Mae: I'm doing my best.

❖

I do have my moments — but they're all weak ones.

❖

You gotta get up early in the morning to catch a fox,
but you have to stay up late at night to get a mink.

❖

Reporter: What types of men do you prefer?
Mae: Just two — domestic and foreign.

❖

It's better to be looked over than overlooked.

❖

Don't ever let any man put anything over you
outside of an umbrella.

❖

A hard man is good to find.

❖

Sex is like bridge: If you don't have a good partner,
you'd better have a good hand.

❖

Marriage is a great institution . . .
but I'm not ready for an institution yet.

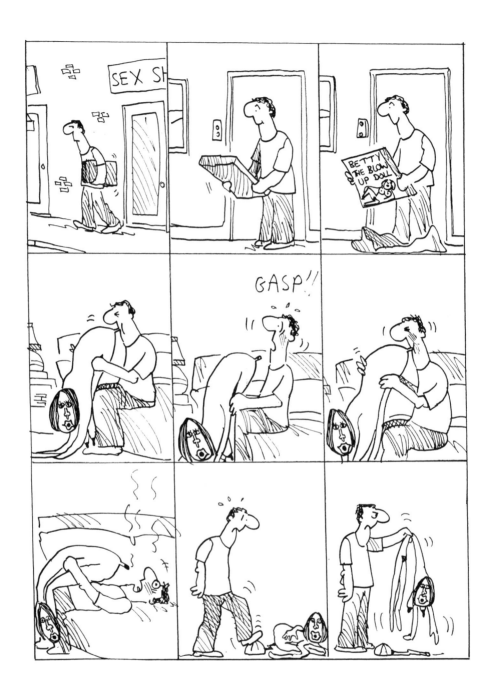

By Tony Husband

BILL AND ZED'S
BAD ADVICE

We've fucked up our lives. Now it's your turn.

Dear Bill and Zed,

I am really scared about asking for advice and wonder if there is a somethingorotherphobia that I can call my condition.

Once I know what to call my debilitating condition I might be able to overcome it by asking for appropriate advice.

Annie xxxxxxxxxxx

ZED: If you tell anyone about your imaginary phobias you will be put in a children's home and your mum won't love you anymore.

Love, Uncle Z.

BILL: Dear Annie,

People should never ask for personal advice, it is an obvious sign of weakness to seek advice from anyone. It is one of the cancers of our age. Of course you are riddled with insecurities, we all are, that is the human condition. But what should be discouraged in others and repressed in one self at all costs is the revealing of these insecurities. I blame the whole industry that has grown up around exploiting people's insecurities, which this column is, sadly, a part of.

Dear Bill & Zed,

Alone, balls balanced on the gleaming gold of an alto sax and liver coiled within, I write to you for some assurance that my fantasy of rogering a pig's liver inserted in a saxophone, whilst my girlfriend blows a long lingering D

note, is not the depraved act she claims it to be. Modern women baffle me. One minute they're knocking back the alcopops giving it all that—promising to fulfill all your sexual fantasies—the next they're self righteously marching out, leaving you, your beloved and the internal organ of some swine high, dry and attracting the flies.

What gives eh? Between you, and me I don't reckon these women can hack it in the real world.

Billy Onions

ZED: You can keep the sax, Billy.
Z

BILL: Dear Mr. Onions,

Look mate, your problem is not women, not even the pigs liver, it's the saxophone. They have got to be the most redundant, useless past every sell by date instrument going. Even at the height of modern Jazz it was the loser's instrument. I mean who was sexier? Miles Davis or Charlie Parker? I bet no chick walked out on Miles, while the Bird couldn't even get up, always being so strung out on horse.

Ditch the sax and get an accordion. Women will see you in a different light, and when they do, you will see them to be wonders of God's creation they truly are.

Yours,
The happy accordionist

Dear Bill & Zed,

Last evening an incident occurred in my house that has left me absolutely baffled with regard to the parameters of what is and isn't acceptable in the ideal of modern parenting.

My five-year-old daughter was refusing to go to bed; bouncing off the walls, screaming, running around and generally destroying the Zen like atmosphere that I had spent the day mindfully cultivating.

I am an extremely patient man, but I do have my limits. So when my enjoyment of Charlie Dimmock's unsupported breasts jiggling on a UKTV Gold rerun was threatened, I understandably snapped. I snatched at the first thing to hand —Mr. Snuffles, my little un's fluffy white kitten—and in my rage ripped its right front leg off.

Breathing heavily, my frenzy escalated to a point whereby I ended up tearing a mouthful of flesh from the stricken beast's dismembered limb. Funnily enough it tasted exactly like the boiled guinea pig I tasted a few months back.

Anyhow, talk about an over reaction; my daughter starts screaming and my wife begins to tremble, prior to projectile vomiting straight onto the ribcage of the toppled tripod pussy.

Basically the rest of the evening was ruined for me. Not only had I missed Ms Dimmock's delights, but I am now in the familial dog house. And for what?

When I was a kid my neighbours had a cat that lost a leg after being run over by a car. It learned to live with it. At least I didn't throw the cat into a sack and flatten it beneath the wheels of my Ford Mondeo. Jesus!!

My question to you two is this; do you think parental wisdom been overrun by political correctness and the opinion of lily-livered, daytime sofa sitting, TV liberals?

Yours with a toothpick

Dr Peter Steinway

ZED: Children need boundaries, boundaries with barbed wire on them. And spanking, lots of spanking, yes. Public schools, yes, public schools, public buggery and public mutual masturbation, yes, and public toilets, everything. Flashing on the train to Waterloo, everything …

You tell them Dr Steinway! Pillar of the establishment!

You tell them!

Politically correct Judge Z with his cock out, wanking in The Old Bailey as he lets the cops off for murder once again.

BILL: Dear Doc,

As far as I'm concerned kids should be allowed to do what ever they want, whenever they want, with whomever they want. I'm almost into double figures on the fathering front, so I know what I'm talking about. As for daytime TV, I have never watched it thus have no opinions about it.

There is something about the tone of your letter that makes me feel it was written almost 10 years ago. The jiggle of Charlie Dimmock's unsupported breasts and carping on about political correctness, were tied old subjects at the turn off the millennium. Next you will be trying to revive those staple topics of chattering class chitchat, from a few years back — 'Are Polish plumbers any good? And 'is reality TV taking over the world?'

Get with it man and help me introduce honour killing into middle class white culture before it is already last years, crime of choice.

Yours,
Bill

Dear Bill and Zed,

I'm considering redecorating. Have you any advice?

Yello

ZED: Don't let the bitch anywhere near your shed.

Z.

BILL: Dear Yello,

I could wax lyrical about my shed for the rest of this issue of the *Idler*, but I will restrain myself. On the subject of decorating — don't bother, one of the great things about sheds is they don't never need it.

Bill

Dear Bill and Zed,

I notice that people are always asking for advice whilst selfishly assuming you have no problems of your own.

Whilst I understand you do court these questions of anguish for the purposes of taking up a few amusing pages in the *Idler* magazine I also felt it might be nice if you could dispose of any bad vibes or feeling by passing on any issues you might need help or advice with?

Or would there be a danger of turning the thing into a problem co-operative and you relinquishing creative balance?

RT

ZED: Mr RT,

How jolly considerate of you, thank you so much.

I am however, feeling rather chipper at the moment. And if I do ever come across any problems in this weary vale, it's usually nothing that a bottle or two of good Scotch, a fine stick or a knife can't resolve.

Rape, murder, alcohol!

That's the way to do it!

Professor Z

BILL: Dear RT,

Well as it happens I do have a small problem of my own. On the various occasions over the past few months when I have been indulging in the pleasures of onanism, I have found that my mind, instead of focussing on my own tried and tested internal blue movie, has begun to stray into making mental notes for my work schedule for the week or the weekend's shopping list.

Bill

Dear Bill and Zed,

We have finally decided to make some use of the bit of garden in back of our house but we cannot come to an agreement as to what to plant. I favour planting petunias whilst my wife Mabel is arguing strongly for cucumbers. On the other hand her father Chip won't hear of anything but fennel or ferns or anything that begins with an 'f'. Could you possible help us to work out a compromise that we can all live with?

Yours
Wally Greensward

ZED: Why not redesignate your gardening plot into a local dogging area. Then you, the father-in-law, the Mrs. and the kids can all get down to some good old-fashioned family fun with your friends and neighbours.

Problem solved, jolly pokey fun for everyone!

I'm sure Mr. *'community activities for everyone'* Bill and his kids would love to join you!

BILL: Dear Walter,

Dogging, Ah those were the days. I'm coming over all wistful just thinking about it. 'A family that dogs together is a family that…' I can't quite remember what my old uncle Arthur used to say. Anyways whatever it was has always made me feel nostalgia for those long ago endless summer nights up on the heath at the back of our small town.

As for gardening — don't.

Bill

Dear Bill and Zed,

I've developed a strange obsession with traditional English folk music and my friends are starting to worry about me. Previously a Fred Perry man, my jumpers now have a distinctly nautical theme, and I can only sing 'Froggy Went a Wooing' in the shower instead of my usual stirring Oasis anthems.

Beer only tastes good from engraved pewter tankards with glass bottoms, and my knowledge of obscure Real Ales has steadily multiplied. Now I know my Crippledick 2000 from my Oatey Badger's Breath, but unfortunately my waistline has expanded so that it now hangs neatly over my stylish corduroy trousers.

Things came to a head last week while supporting my local football team. Instead of 'Come on you Blues!' I could only sing, 'Fol de rol de fiddle-I ro', and some fellow supporters beat me senseless with a breezeblock and shaved off my beard with a rusty Gillette.

I feel like I'll never be able to hold my head up with pride again until this Demon is exorcised. I've memorized all the major Childe ballads and I'm spending a fortune on batteries for my electronic jumper de-fluffer. Help!

Johnny the Jolly Rover
who a wooing did go

ZED: Dear Johnny, nothing that a jag, a Harley Davidson, a little yellow cravat can't resolve. Your au-pair looks pretty hot as well.

Mid life crisis, old boy. Embrace!

BILL: Dear Jonny,

A short, sharp shock is what you need, to put a stop to this folk music and real ale folly. A mid life crisis is certainly in order, but when choosing your own mid life crisis you can never be too careful. I've never been too keen on the Harley Davidson route but my fellow Zen master shows taste when recommending the yellow silk cravat and having a go on the au-pair, but why not try evolving something original, never been done before. Let us know how it goes.

Yours,
Bill

Dear Bill and Zed,

I have an overwhelming feeling something's fundamentally wrong with society. Is it just me, or am I on to something?

Love
Suzanne

ZED: Dear Suzanne, why not meet me in The Shifty Arms later, where I can pay you lots of attention and discuss your existential quandaries further.

Trust me, I know everything and am pretty sexy for an old bloke.

Suzanne, such a pretty name.

Man of the world Z

BILL: Suzanne, You are nothing but a slut and a whore. You told me that I gave you all the meaning your life needed. That our one night with me was better than any other night you ever had. That us together would make your life complete and now you are writing into agony columns and flirting outrageously with my cheap and low life colleague. 🐚

CONVERSATIONS

Damien Hirst: 'Love's Paradox (Surrender or Autonomy – Separateness as a Precondition for Connection)', 2007
This piece from Beyond Belief, Hirst's recent show, was inspired by Esther Perel's book
Image courtesy of the artist

IN CONVERSATION WITH
ESTHER PEREL

Tom Hodgkinson gets it on with the New York sex therapist

LAST YEAR ESTHER PEREL PUBLISHED A BOOK CALLED *Mating in Captivity: Reconciling the Erotic and the Domestic*. The work asks why sex can often disappear when couples get cosy and domesticated. It has touched a nerve and been published in twenty countries. Here she discusses love's paradox and ways to bring a sense of playfulness back into our relationships.

IDLER: You are saying that sex is better when there is *less* intimacy. It's when you keep your distance and you don't merge: that's when things are more erotic ... men's magazines and women's magazine encourage the idea of sex as something you have to work at, like a competitive sport ... I tend to think: what's wrong with lying in the olive groves all day with a bottle of wine and your beloved? You also say that people are very lonely today ... we ask of our partner the things that a whole village would have supplied in the past.

ESTHER PEREL: The British were the first to look at the book from a particular angle which shaped it and defined it very differently. When the *Observer* came out, the *Daily Mail*, *Telegraph* — they all began to talk about this phenomenon: what happens to this generation that has egalitarian ideals in its head, contraception in its hand, lots of pre-marital sexual experience and comes to

a committed relationship with an expectation of sexual fulfilment, and finds itself with very little desire for it or at least for their partner ... they don't understand it because they came with an expectation sexuality to be an essential dimension of their relationship. Many of these couples are not in troubled relationships: they are very good couples, but whose desire is flagging. They complain of the listlessness of their sex lives; they sometimes want more and they always want better, and what they long for is the sense of connection, renewal and playfulness that sexuality used to afford them ... a certain intensity that gives them a feeling of being alive. Not the act itself. I'm interested in the erotic dimension: what helps people feel alive inside their relationshp and in life in general. In that sense, the erotic is the cultivation of pleasure for its own sake. It's not measurable. The book was much less about sex *per se* and more about the ambiguities of desire and the quest for the erotic.

IDLER: What factors do you blame for us having got into this position?

EP: I don't know that I blame factors. I think that the idea of reconciling eroticism and domesticity in one relationship is new and brings with it a set of challenges. The idea that in the same relationship we want to experience grounding, meaning and continuity, as well as transcendence and adventure and novelty, is contradictory. We want respectability, children, family life, economic support, and at the same time we want that person to be our best friend and our confidant and our passionate lover. It is not always the lack of closeness that stifles desire but sometimes too much closeness.

IDLER: You say that the partner is more fanciable when you see them in the distance and you get that glimpse.

EP: I've asked this question in ten countries, give me a moment when you are most drawn to your partner? They say, when he plays with the kids, when she's giving a talk at work, when I see him play his instrument, when she does something that she's passionate and intense about. But it's not when they're looking at each other 10 cm from each other, no longer able to distinguish the countours of the other, and not when they're that far when they can no longer distinguish them either. It's when they are at a certain distance, from where they can look at each other as separate people involved in their own thing ... for which I don't have to take care of them and their otherness is accentuated, they're talking with a third person, they're in a club, other people are looking at them ... there is a shift in perception in which what is usually so familiar is once again mysterious and still unknown.

IDLER: Which makes sense, because for most people because the most intense period sexually of a relationship is the beginning, when you're still separate individuals.

EP: But it's in the structure. You don't have to cultivate the separateness: it's already built in. That's why in the beginning it's much easier for people to combine love and desire, than afterwards. It's not intimacy *per se* that is problematic, we seek that and I'm not an intimacy-basher by any means, what I am saying is that while love wants that kind of closeness, and love is about having and knowing, desire thrives on the elusive and needs a certain distance to thrive, and is about wanting, not having. In that sense it needs air — like fire needs air — and many relationships today find it hard to maintain air between them, in part because of the romantic idea that believes in sharing everything, in cultivating transparency, and basicaslly in eradicating distances, and I do believe that desire needs a certain amount of tension, and difference.

IDLER: I like the idea of a more old-fashioned household. I read in books of Tudor history things like: 'I visited my lady's chamber.' The woman and the man of the house appeared to have their own completely separate lives, their own courts. They would come together at mealtimes. They had joint projects but separate bedrooms. That to me is a sexy idea ...

EP: In Jewish law, that's what people do: they sleep separately and they don't touch. Then they go to the ritual bath and they have two weeks where they are invited to be luscious and sexual.

IDLER: That's an ancient idea?

EP: That is the contemporary idea of Orthodox Judaism. That is the way that sexuality is regulated in traditional Jewish law.

IDLER: Another great point that you make in the book is that some element of formality can actually be quite sexy ... when you're first going out with someone, you make an appointment, go out or for dinner, and there's probably going to be sex at the end of it. But established couples would find making a date for sex a difficult idea.

EP: Unless they play it ... a certain kind of over-familiarity can numb desire. If we share everything it becomes harder to maintain a sense of lustfulness, it's too much of a taboo, we don't want sex in the family, therefore maintaining a separation or boundaries or privacy are elements that can nurture desire. On the other hand, we do live in a nuclear family, not everyone wants to have separate quarters ... but the idea is that sexuality can be a playing field, a theatre, a stage, that actually allows us playfully to go against what we do in the kitchen between six and eight.

IDLER: Didn't Benjamin Franklin say that once a month you should take your wife away to a hotel and treat her like a prostitute?

EP: There was one couple I saw who was doing so. I don't advise, I describe what I know people do: the idea is that people can be more playful, more seductive, erotic, more pleasure-bound, in a space that is outside of their home. They can bring out different parts of their personality when they are not in the space where there are no children and carers and responsible adults. And for some people, that's the hotel. I don't advise it but I understand what it is.

IDLER: Are you French?

EP: I'm originally Flemish-Belgian.

IDLER: Right ... it's just that when I've visited France, they all seem to have mistresses ... affairs seem to be more a part of the culture than England. Having affairs would seem to be a solution. Do your couples do that?

EP: I think people engaging in extramarital relations in the US is no different from France. It's the attitudes that are different, not the statistics. Wherever women have more power and economic independence, their numbers are not that far off from men, either. The reasons for the affairs, and what they look for in them, may be quite different. In France there is a certain kind of understanding, and for the Italians, too, that indeed there may not be one relationship where you can find all. But you don't therefore separate. What I think is the difference between the Anglo-Saxon world and the Latin world has to do with the level of indvidualism. Some societies develop greater tolerance for divorce, while the other societies develop greater tolerance for sexual infidelity.

IDLER: Does one go for a serial monogamy or stay with your main formal possibly sex-free relationship ...

EP: And not even necessarily sex-free ... the idea that you go outside just because you don't have it at home, no! The life outside home might have nothing to do with home ... life brought you something that doesn't exist at home but not that you even looked for at home either. The idea that infidelities are always troubles or symptoms of disappointment in the relationship is an easy supposition but it doesn't necessarily bear true. And in societies where affairs are more tolerated, it's not that they think affairs are a great idea, it's just that they don't think they warrant destroying the family. Because they see the marriage as being not just two individuals … there are a lot of other people involved and you don't drag them into it.

IDLER: You could argue that there's something self-indulgent about the ease and the willingness with which people divorce.

EP: Yes … you could say that, or you could say that people who divorce are greater idealists, because when they divorce they don't question the model, they just think they chose the wrong person.

IDLER: The triumph of hope over experience.

EP: The divorce can be seen as an expression of how tenaciously they hold on to the model.

IDLER: But don't you find that people fall into the same patterns in their second or thrid marriage?

EP: Well, in the States first marriage, have a 50% divorce rate and second marriages have a 65% divorce rate! What does this say?

IDLER: So it's not the other person who is at fault, it's either you or the institution. Now, in some cultures, and in history, prostitution is tolerated, as it was for example in medieval Florence, where there were these bath-houses, where you went for sex with your wife. The bath-houses also had prostitutes. It was kind of accepted by the priests because they thought it prevented a greater sin, which was infidelity. That's another way of dealing with the problem.

EP: You don't have to go to the Middle Ages. I was in Brazil last month.

IDLER: The sex hotels!

EP: Besides the sex hotels, I went to a place that until a few years ago was called The Silver Pussy. To that club the young man was brought by his brother or by his father, to be initiated by an experienced women. And at the same time as he was being initiated by her, he was protecting the virginity of the good girl he would marry later. Now he's not needing to go that club any more because the good girl is supposed to have pre-marital sex with him, and after she has a child, he's not supposed to go there any more either because they're supposed to cultivate desire as an expression of love in their own relationship. When people ask, are there societies where people have more sex, I say, yes: the ones where people have more children and the ones where women have less power. Yes! One, because sexuality becomes one of their main powers, and two because they don't have the possibility of saying 'no'. It's in emancipated Western societies where sex is merely a matter of desire, it's no longer operated by reproduction, it's not sustained by power distribution, so it's a question of: if I'm in the mood and you're in the mood and it happens to be at the same time. Therefore it requires that we cultivate desire and seduction and erotic engagement in the context of our own home in ways we never had to do before. It's not enough to say, I feel like it, and she obliges. He has to elicit her interest, he has to invite her and he never had to do that at home. Especially not when he goes to the prostitute.

IDLER: St. Paul says that the woman can ask for sex from the man if he doesn't feel like it, as well. It was the marriage debt, and either partner had to pay the debt if the other felt like it. Isn't there an argument that people should go through with it even if they don't feel like it?

EP: I think you can make the argument: desire doesn't always precede experience. Sometimes it comes with it. Especially as we get older, we don't always expect sexual desire but we may have a desire for sex. The difference is that the sexual desire is internally prompted but the desire for sex is a response to motivations that are not always sexual in nature, such as: it would be nice, we'll feel good afterwards, he'll be in a better mood, I'll be relaxed. Give her the experience and then the desire will follow. She starts by thinking, why not?

IDLER: How do you get them into that state?

EP: They need to understand that this can be a pathway to desire. There is something very limiting in only seeing sexual desire as only physically based response … she may want to engage in sex because she's having a fantastic conversation, because he's making her laugh, because he cooked her favourite meal. It has nothing to do with what's going on between her legs. That is one of the fundamental difference in pathways of desire between men and women. And that's why I make the disctinction between sexual desire and desire for sex.

IDLER: So it's a question of seeing sexuality as part of a whole thing rather than one little isolated element.

EP: Absolutely. And definitely for women, desire operates on a continuum.

IDLER: You talk in the book about a lack of desire being equally felt by the man and woman. But anecdotally in my experience, it's the men complaining that the women are not up for it. The men's desire hasn't gone away.

EP: There's a number of things going on there. I think that for dads with young children, go back and read the chapter on parenthood. When women enter into motherhood they often find it harder to fnd the woman behind the mother, to reconnect with their permission for pleasure in the context of being responsible and loving for others.

IDLER: There's a sort of saintliness...

EP: It's an inhibition about experiencing the selfishness that is inherent in desire, when you have the role of being carer of three little kids.

IDLER: Not really compatible.

EP: And many mothers will tell you that it really changes when the youngest one goes to kindergarten.

IDLER: Well, I'm looking forward to that stage.

EP: There is suddenly a space that opens up and they can finally turn to themselves.

IDLER: D H Lawrence said that people divorce too much over this issue … people should just wait for the paths to flow together. The thing will change of its own accord without you having to put much effort into it.

EP: No. I think that there are things that happen when people have young children. Their need for safety and stability magnify and they start to suppress the side of them that is more adventurous and freedom-seeking, because the children become the adventure. For many women, the idea that they can engage in the selfishness of desire whie they are mired in a role of motherly love, carteaking and being responsible feels like a conflict and that's why they are much more able to connect wth that part when they are outisde the house, on a weekend, on a trip, but not in the room next door. Then there is the fact that their entire ertoic energy is alive and well but is all directed onto the children, and the couple goes on with the same-old same-old. It is totally channeled into the children and at some point couples need to know how to bring some of that erotic energy back into the relationship. I disagree with D H Lawrence that you just do nothing. I think it's true that desire will ebb and flow, but at the same time there are things that you can do.

IDLER: So you need to put some thought into this.

EP: Yes. I think that committed sex is pre-meditated sex. It's wilful and it's intentional. It doesn't just happen. You make it happen. It's seduction. The reality of society seems to be that the man is still interested in sex and the woman loses desire. But in the therapist's office, we tend to see equal numbers. If a woman loses desire, it tends to be so expected that he's not going to bring her to therapy. But if a man loses desire, you may be sure they'll be in the therapist's office very soon, because the woman will worry about it, she will wonder about what's going on, she will want him to come with her to address this. So I can't only see it as an attribute of the woman. It tends to be more an attribute of the primary parent, the person whose sense of self has been totally invaded, if you like, by caring for the children.

IDLER: So it's the mothering that's incompatible with eroticism. What do people do in relationships where this is not a problem?

EP: The way I phrase it is to say that what eroticism thrives on — the novel, the mysterious, the unpredictable — is what family life defends against. Family life thrives in an atmosphere of consistency and routine, and those are killers of desire. But couples who have it can create an erotic space for themselves, in which they meet as adults, in which they go out — not to talk about their kids in which they get dressed up, they go dancing. They remain playfully and seductively engaged with each other. Even if for a few years they have much less frequent sex, it's not a matter of how often they have orgasm or intercourse, it's really a question of how they remain erotically engaged with each other. They are not people who are constantly stroking their children and haven't touched each other in God knows how long. They don't just invite the children to come into bed with them and linger around in bed with them, but also find moments to be with each other. They are people who don't wait till 11.30 at night when they are beat but sometimes they decide to meet for lunch when they are dressed up and awake.

IDLER: I sometimes wonder whether bed is not the best place for it.

EP: Oh, bed is often the last place. It's often the place where they discuss all the realities of life, it's the place where they've already experienced a lot of rejection. I often tell people that they should look for other flat surfaces in their house!

IDLER: In the maypole tradition, the dancing was followed by sex in the woods. I can't quite imagine that happening nowadays.

EP: Because we're supposed to do it at home because now that we have the permission to be wild in our house. But we realise that maybe being wild in our house isn't such an easy thing to do. And that many of us can be wilder when we leave the confines of this responsible, serious place that is called home.

IDLER: But then the home is where we have most control: it could be an anarchic wild domain if we chose it to be.

EP: And the people who have the spark are the people who know how to invite ceremony, ritual, playfulness—inside their own home. And that's how they create their own sexual space, fantasy space, then they don't feel like they're in their home.

IDLER: A magical element?

EP: Yes. It's interesting how when people make a nice dinner, they set the table, they light candles, they cook nice food, open a nice bottle of wine. But with sex they imaagine that they can finish the dishes, turn off the television, go upstairs and just get going! Without any ritual or ceremony, nothing to anticipate. In order to want sex, it needs to be sex worth wanting. And it's not always worth wanting, the way we do it.

IDLER: Another thing that strikes me is how little we dance nowadays. In the 18th century, everyone had dancing masters. Dancing was a part of the everyday curriculum for schoolchildren. People danced every night after dinner.

EP: I'm very keen on that. We need to develop pleasure not just in the bed but outside, and dancing and movement, and the sensuality and the physical contact, and the suggestiveness that comes from dancing. And it's usually the middle class that dances the least. If you go to the salsa clubs or the African clubs in New York, the only people who don't dance are the white people, ususally, the white middle class.

IDLER: Well, middle class morality is against things like that: the Puritans banned dancing ... but the more old-fashioned cultures still do it ... in Mexico they don't feel the need to go on holiday because they are celebrating all year round, there are constant festivals and parties, often religious in nature. And that would lead to more sex,

I suppose.

EP: Often it does. Music, movement: you can't dance and be unhappy. It's physical, it engages the senses, and it often invites a certain erotic connection. I look for ways to cultivate that erotic connection that isn't straightforward sex, but that induces the desire for sex. That's the erotic space. It's a space where pleasure is cultivated for its own sake, and sex can happen and often does, but it's not made for sex.

IDLER: So you can't expect to go dancing just once and have sex.

EP: Whatever it is that you choose to do that is physical and playful. With some couples it will be dancing; with others it will be taking hikes on top of the mountains. I tend not to give an explicit prescriptive. Instead I explain the principle. When you are dancing with your partner you are engaging with him in a completely different way than when you are in the hosue thinking about the cleaning, thinking about what has to be done ... You can't dance and think about what you need to do.

IDLER: Isn't there a biological issue? Once women have their beautiful babies there is not such a need to have sex, so what's the point?

EP: No because we all want to be touched. When you say women don't want sex, maybe they're less inclined to genital sex. But that doesn't mean that she can't engage in loads of sexual play. The woman with three young children who hasn't been interested at all—you put a new man in front of her and you'll be surprised by what she will discover in her. I think the transition is more difficult for a woman. It takes longer, between leaving these responsibilities and giving herself permission to enter

"What if it was possible to copy the contents of our minds onto a computer? Copy, not transfer. I would still be walking and talking in the real world, in front of all you. However a digital version of me could also communicate with me, and vice versa. This uploaded self would be a hypotheses based on readings of the neural activity of the brain combined with observations of my behaviour. Just enough to capture the pattern of your identity and not necessarily every single detail of you. This hypotheses is plugged into existing routines for simulating chemical, cellular and hormonal influences on brain activity. It is then animated and placed in a community of other uploaded beings.

"I don't want you to dwell on the feasibility of this. My question is: what do we call these other selves? Whatever term you come up with must be a forward-facing mainstream consumer proposition. Imagine this technology percolating into society much as the mobile phone did. Beginning with a rich executive elite and over time drilling all the way through the demographic bands. We'll discuss your conclusions at sundown."

THE RED MEN
MATTHEW DE ABAITUA

IN ALL GOOD BOOKSTORES 4TH OCTOBER 2007

READ MORE AT
WWW.SNOWBOOKS.COM/THEREDMEN/

inside herself ... she may be less inclined to frequency but that doesn't mean she doesn't remain connected as a sexual being. I've seen women who can't be bothered, who want to be in bed at eight, and one day they stumble upon somebody and suddenly they no longer need to sleep *at all* because they're interested. It's a mental attitude. It's the way desire works. It's amazing also how the same woman who when faced with the fear of loss, that the husband might go elsewhere, can become a voracious vixen. The fear of loss is a powerful aphrodisiac. Because suddenly there is something to want, to reclaim. There is something about insecurity and intensity and exceitement. Unfortunately I would say that passion is commensurate with the amount of uncertainty we can tolerate.

IDLER: So you're arguing for an injection of wildness into the domestic realm.

EP: Maybe not wildness but if you want to cultivate the erotic in your home, then it requires you stay connected to the playful the curious, the novel, the seductive, the longing — all the elements that fuel desire. We basically decide that we are more comfortable living in affectionate, secure coupledom, cosy, but unexciting. We can do that for a good number of years and be OK.

IDLER: The book is coming out in twenty countries, right, and you've just visited half of them on a tour. Which cultures have appeared to you to be the healthiest?

EP: Every country has its own problems and resources. I would like to say Brazil, but Brazil has its own complications. I think the book has had this kind of resonance because it speaks to a modern conundrum. I tapped into something long unspoken.

IDLER: We've been brought up to feel liberated about these things; then we find something's gone wrong.

EP: At first I didn't expect that the book would have such a response worldwide. It was intended as a comment on American sexuality by a foreign therapist.

IDLER: I always assume that other countries are doing it: Brazil is a non-stop sex party, so is France.

EP: Well, England doesn't come from a tradition that understands that kind of seductive playfulness. People there seem to go back and forth between being shy and tongue-tied to being drunk and slobbering all over you.

IDLER: Yes, that's our technique.

EP: British people do not have a self-image as elegant and seductive.

IDLER: But there could be a lot in common back at home, even between cultures that look very different when they're out.

EP: Go to Brazil. You can see that there is a real attention to the erotic in the society at large and I can't imagine that it doesn't enter into the privacy of the people's homes. The country dances, the carnival: they understand ritual, costumes, fantasy. But given all of that, I still think that reconciling the erotic and the domestic is a challenge, period. In any country. And a paradox that you manage, not a problem that you solve with ten techniques.

IDLER: We should be looking at it as a game, not a competitive sport.

EP: For sure. The whole idea for me was to look at the poetics of sex.

Kevin Godley's exuberant response at being offered a bazillion dollars to direct a McDonald's advert.

POP IDLE

Paul Hamilton meets British pop's laidback genius,

Kevin Godley

W hen Kevin Godley, singing drummer with 1970s hit factory 10cc, stopped collaborating with Lol Creme after their 1988 album Goodbye Blue Sky, he hung up his microphone to devote nearly twenty years to directing pop videos. In 2006, however, a new website — gg06.co.uk — appeared, quietly heralding his return to songwriting and singing. The new material was produced with 10cc bassist (and friend for fifty — count 'em! — years) Graham Gouldman.

The Idler met the sunny Mr Godley on a rainy day in Soho to find out if his and Graham's new songs are more than, to quote one of his biggest hits, just a silly phase they're going through . . .

IDLER: I'll begin with the opening lines of one of your records: 'Are you bored? Are you jaded? Has all the enthusiasm faded?'

KEVIN GODLEY: That rings a bell. What's that one? Was it from *Consequences*? No, it's *L*; 'This Sporting Life'. *L* is my favourite Godley & Creme album.

IDLER: Oddly, Lol has said he hates *L* — he calls it doomy, morbid. But then you've gone on record insisting *Consequences* is 'shite, shite, shite' whilst Lol insists it's a pinnacle of his life.

KG: It's not shite. It's 'More Is More'. Wrong time, wrong place. The 9/11 of concept albums. Re musical tastes ... Well, in hindsight, that's where our tastes diverge. I've always loved words whereas Lol was more into musicianship and sound. The music on *Consequences* was two-thirds instrumental — not a lot to do for a budding wordsmith. *L, Freeze Frame, Birds Of Prey* and, more so, the GG06 material rely heavily on words. There is some valuable stuff on *Consequences* but it was our Heaven's Gate. Out of the time frame that's a pretty good film, but it's hard to separate from the moment, yes? There are many grand buildings out there but some of them are follies. Folly Berserk. It was one of those projects that drove at its own pace because we didn't quite know what we were doing. Unspoken brief: 'Stay In The Studio Longer Than Anybody Else, stay as stoned as possible and hang with Peter Cook'. Actually it was a musical comedy version of *An Inconvenient Truth*. Final comment on The Big C: In my opinion ... We were playing to our weaknesses instead of our strengths.

IDLER: A favourite line on *Consequences* is when Peter drones, 'We musicians flourish in an atmosphere of studied chaos. It's taken me *years* to achieve this mess.'

KG: Yes! It's true. You should see my desk.

IDLER: Peter Cook-type question for you:

What's the worst job you've ever had?

KG: I've never had a job.

IDLER: You'll be 62 this year, fast approaching retirement age, and yet you choose now to return to music-making.

KG: I can't even consider the notion of retirement since I don't actually work as such. I've got nothing to retire *from*. I do a bit of this and a bit of that. My life's been a series of lucky accidents — lucky for me, unlucky for practically anybody else. I suppose if I played the game properly I'd have been a graphic designer since that's what I was trained for at art school. The extraordinary thing about the baby boomer art school years is that it instilled, in everyone there, the belief that anything was possible — and not exclusively in art and design but in every medium.

IDLER: Your songs are always written in collaboration — and creative partnerships have always fascinated me, how they go about it, how their minds meet. Galton and Simpson, when writing *Steptoe and Son* and *Hancock*, would sit and go through each line of a script together. They said that if they got stuck at some point in the script they would sit there in silence, unable to do proceed until the next line eventually emerged. Whereas Perry and Croft, the *Dad's Army* writers, would have a meeting where they'd discuss the plotlines for the next series of episodes then write them separately. However, such was the style of the show, years later they were unable to tell who had written which episode. OK, I'm talking about comedy scriptwriters rather than songwriters but what was the *modus operandi* of you and Lol Creme? Was it a clear-cut operation whereby one does the lyrics and one provides the tunes, like Elton John and Bernie Taupin?

KG: We were together for twenty-seven years in a highly creative partnership and, for the most part, we operated as two halves of the same brain. We both thought the same way about whatever we were trying to accomplish but we had subtly different things to bring to the table. We always covered each other. If one wasn't coming up with a lyric that was required, the other would do it, because our heads were in the same zone. It was more a split personality than two separate people. It was Two People Against The World — we had very individual, unique ideas, and it was very intense for a long time. We were busy boys.

IDLER: What did Mrs Godley and Mrs Creme make of all this? Or were they too busy on their own concept album?

KG: Two blues albums.

IDLER: Do you ever play your own records? Do you look back?

KG: Occasionally I do, but just to remind me if they're any good and if they're how I remember them. Recently, I played 'I Pity Inanimate Objects' from, um, *Freeze Frame* and I remembered how and why we actually did that. The idea was driven by a new piece of equipment called a harmoniser. It's used in studios all the time these days as a corrective device to get performances in tune, but this early version came with a keyboard. You could put a sound through a harmoniser and if you wanted an instrument or voice to hit a certain note that it hadn't, you could play that note on the keyboard. So we got to thinking, 'Let's forget about singing for the moment. What happens if I vocalize these words in a monotone — do an entire song on one note — and get Lol to play my vocal on the harmoniser keyboard?' That was the experiment. It worked pretty well. Predated Cher's digital gurglings by a few years. I don't know where the lyric came from. Maybe because the harmoniser was inanimate.

You know, the key to the writing process is finding your way in, bringing the stuff that's in peripheral hearing into focus. You're always aiming to get inside the song/story/film so it can write you instead of the the other way round. You're always trying to build something solid out of invisible and ghostly raw materials. Did I just say that?

IDLER: It wasn't me … After a few years in relative obscurity, you and Lol scored a Top Five single in 1981 with 'Under Your Thumb', a record stripped of your trademarks. No massed vocal harmonies, no exotic instrumentation, no crackpot unexpected middle-eights. It's a very straight story performed by a solo vocal and a synthesizer. It's almost a demo in comparison to your past productions. There wasn't even a video.

KG: Yeah, we were on *Top Of The Pops* with smoke billowing out of my sleeves. Why was it a hit? A hit is something everyone wants to like, that's why it's a hit. Despite ourselves we hit that nerve. What happened was we got a little home studio, a 16-track machine, set up in Lol's house. Thought it'd be fun to do it ourselves, and Lol could engineer it on a basic level. He was tinkering about with this synthesizer one day with a rhythm box chugging along when he came up with this riff. I said, 'That's cool', and started singing something along with it — as you do. You see, if you haven't got a sonic template of 'How You Should Sound' then you're excited by anything that seems to work. That track succeeded at a very simple level — it didn't require a great deal of window dressing. Our sense of it was the more layers we took off, the more skeletal it became and the better it got.

IDLER: It's puzzling how the quality of a song can be obscured or judged by the context of who's singing it and their attendant image and personal mythology. If, say, Bob Dylan had written and recorded your song 'Joey's Camel' there'd be endless reams written by pop sleuths, examining the lyrics for insights into Dylan's stand on Zionism or chipping away for subversive, coded messages. By the same token, had it been you two who made Dylan's *Desire* album it would've been dismissed as 'clever dick eggheads don sombreros'.

KG: Yeah, pop culture/music is driven equally by its own mythology and its visual impact. It always has been, going all the way back to Elvis and even Sinatra. It's hard to separate the music from the artist's personality and the hype — what they do, how they look, who they are perceived to be. It really annoys me when people discuss the music of the '70s — 'Oh yeah, man — Bolan, Bowie, Roxy, punk, Slade' — and 10cc are always excluded. This is because of our total lack of Bad Boy Rebel credentials and, for some reason, not really taking care of our visual presentation.

IDLER: Which is strange for ex-art students.

KG: Exactly. We were *not* exciting to look at. We may have sounded like 400 Maniacs From Hollywood but we were Four Wankers From Manchester and therein lies the dichotomy. Most artists who are Huge and — inverted commas — 'Significant' are so not merely because of what they're singing about, it's because of their personal mythology — whether it's actually true or not.

IDLER: Lemmy from Motörhead has this speed-freak king of metal image but he's only really addicted to pub quiz machines.

KG: Right. Consequently, 10cc are a blip on the graph. I'm not bitter about it; I just never understood it until recently…

IDLER: Speaking of image and unrestrained outrageousness, I've seen 10cc miming to 'Life Is A Minestrone' on *Top Of The Pops* where you're wearing a jumper with your face crocheted on the front. What the hell is going on?

KG: It was a present from a fashion designer friend called Paul Howie. I thought it was better-looking than me, really.

IDLER: It garnered some positive comments on the Youtube noticeboard.

KG: What — 'Where can I get a Kevin Godley jumper?' Ohhhhh God ... Not *quite* Che Guevara though, is it? No, what we're really talking about is the Tyranny Of Cool.

IDLER: In your 1981 song 'Snack Attack' you rapped, 'Gimme sausage, eggs, beans and chips/Pancakes, clambakes, fondue and dips/And sauces, horses, seventeen courses of barbecued beef and asparagus tips'. By the end of the '80s, however, you had become a vegetarian and got involved in environmental pressure groups like Ark. What brought this about?

KG: I became a vegetarian because, um ... I used to live in a house [*Tara House, five glass pyramids in Chertsey, Surrey. Previous tenant: Keith Moon*] which had a swimming pool, and every year, as in the classic series one Sopranos scene, a family of ducks would come and stay in the pool and then leave. One year the ducks flew away but left their smallest, a little duckling, behind. So we caught him, put him in a box with small holes in, took him to a bird sanctuary outside Chertsey. Phew, saved his life. Then we went out to Mr Chow's and had crispy duck. We thought, 'Hang on a minute!' It was like the veil had been lifted. I'd never been a huge fan of meat anyway — I just liked the sauces. So we just decided, 'Let's just not eat meat for a bit and see how we go.' That was thirty years ago ... I'm still a vegetable.

I became involved with the environmental pressure group ARK through meeting Chrissie Hynde who is far more extreme and radical than I am but wanted to reach ordinary people. A very diverse group of people got together to do something practical to change the way things are. For that time — late '80s — we did pretty well until the Ark Organisation tore itself apart. Leadership squabbles. A real shame. What they were fighting for then is top priority all over the world now.

IDLER: I never met the chap but I couldn't imagine Lol being sympathetic to this change in you.

KG: No. He took it with a huge pinch of salt.

IDLER: Was this a significant crack in the relationship?

KG: It was. I mean, we lived in each others' minds for 27 years, so when, a few years before Ark, I was asked to shoot the Fashion Aid show at the Albert Hall I was nervous because I'd never done anything without Lol before. I had to take some time out to do it because I was on my own, it was quite daunting. I don't think it helped the Godley & Creme situation. But with that, and with Ark, I found that I *could* do it and it was liberating not having to ask someone else's opinion. I now think two people working on one thing, both covering the same bases, is unnatural but that's the way we were so used to being for so long and, for better or worse, that's the way it went. I found I rather liked being in control of my own destiny and we very gradually drifted apart.

IDLER: What was Lol's reaction to your Fashion Aid film? Hissy fit?

KG: Sorry, what's that? 'Pissy feet'? Yes, he pissed on my feet.

IDLER: When you two split, it must have seemed like a divorce. Did you go through a period of denial, as one might undergo

Keep On Fucking: Godley's remembrance of those tender, intimate moments.
From his and Creme's semi-memoir The Fun Starts Here *(1981).*

following a marital break-up? You know, being unable to play the records you made, see the videos you directed together, seeing nothing of positive value in any of it?

KG: No, I was and am proud of what we did and always will be. Even *Consequences*. I know I sometimes say there are faults with it —

IDLER: Yeah, it's too short for one thing.

KG: Yeah, let's make it a *six* album set! Retool up the Gizmotron. A seven disc DVD package. There should be 14 more of them. One for every month in the studio. *Consequences II* ... God ...

IDLER: Was there a terrible G & C video in your opinion — one wear you're gawping through your fingers?

KG: No, for the simple reason that we always chose the best directors — ourselves! (*Laughs*) Unfortunately, Lol wasn't into being in front of the camera — you can see that in 'Wedding Bells'. Strange, because he's an outgoing guy. When we were at art college we did a two-man show where he was all over the stage. He could've been a stand-up comedian at one point; very, very giving to the audience. But, somehow, as I was stepping out from behind the drumkit and taking the lead vocals he was doing the opposite.

Peter Cook, Kevin Godley and Lol Creme working flat out on their 1977 triple-album 'Consequences'.
A full year spent in its recording, its total world sales could be counted on the fingers of a leper's foot. It was such
an outrageous financial disaster, G & C would be cast into the commercial wilderness for five long years.

IDLER: Are you ever recognised by Will Young or Keane or these other young scamps whose vids you direct? Do they sing a burst of 'You make me wanna cryyyyyyyyyyyyyyyyyyyy?'

KG: No, taxi drivers do that: 'Hey, you're the one with all the faces, right?' — 'Yeah, I'm just changing into the little girl now.' They always remember 'Cry'. It's like Michael Caine — wherever he goes there's always someone shouting 'You're only supposed to blow the bloody doors off!' The faces are my doors.

IDLER: Have you ever had Bono come up and say, "'The Sweetest Thing' is good but we'll never top 'Wide Boy?'"

KG: No, because he's a very honest guy. Heard an intriguing story from Sean O'Hagan, though. Apparently 'Rubber Bullets' was a kind of anthem/rallying cry in Northern Ireland during the troubles. *How?* It was about an American prison riot. People home in on what they want from a song — the words 'rubber' and 'bullets'.

IDLER: It was initially banned by the BBC for that reason, although the year before, Lou Reed's 'Walk On The Wild Side' snuck through with its explicit drug and blowjob references intact.

KG: If you're going to do something wrong, do it right.

IDLER: How choosy are you in respect of the songs you make videos of or the companies you make adverts for? Have you ever turned commissions down on ethical grounds?

KG: I would definitely turn down McDonalds or some other corporation that offends me, yes.

IDLER: You couldn't be bought at any price?

KG: No. Well ... Twenty quid and I'm yours! (*Laughter*) I don't really do commercials that often because I don't like the business. I'm the one in the Pepsi pre-production meeting saying, 'Guys, it's only a drink.' They look at me as though I'm crazy 'cos it's a way of life to them. To me it's not. Lol and I were asked by Herb Alpert — of 'Tijuana Brass' fame — to come up with a commercial for his new fragrance. We ended up passing because we couldn't take it seriously.

IDLER: What was it called?

KG: 'Trumpet.' (*Gales of laughter*) Who in their right mind would buy a fragrance called Trumpet? 'The great smell ... of Trumpet.' (*Parp!*)

IDLER: How many videos do you make a year on average?

KG: Not many. The business has changed radically because of Youtube. If you want to watch a video, click on Youtube and nine times out of ten it's going to be there. Which is fine, but record companies are rubbing their hands in glee because 'Oh, Cheapo is in!' (*laughs*) The record business at the moment is shooting itself very slowly in the foot. It ignored the digital medium when it arrived; it's unwilling to develop new talent; it's not geared to expanding and adapting. The upshot is people are losing interest. If they can't find something to excite them they'll look elsewhere — and it might not always be at music. Music has become only one of a number of ways to entertain whereas (*stentorian American voice:*) back in the golden years —

IDLER: — it was a Way Of Life.

KG: Hearing the new Beatles song or the next Dylan track was the best moment of the week. You'd queue outside a record booth, waiting to stick those headphones on and hear it. 'Oh, man!' Then you'd race

home to wear it death on the Dansette.

IDLER: Yeah, settle down, grandad. What tickles your pickle at the moment?

KG: Arcade Fire, Tom Waits, Razorlight, Corinne Bailey Rae, a band called OK Go. You must've seen it. They've got a video where they're all on treadmills. Spectacular performance. Locked-off camera. They're lip-synching whilst performing a genius piece of choreography. Best video ever.

IDLER: Ever since you were a child you wanted to make feature films.

KG: Still do. Haven't done it yet. I've written two and they haven't been made yet. Maybe I'm not driven enough. Maybe I haven't got a 'pitch personality'.

IDLER: Go on, pitch your film to me.

KG: 'I've written this film, read it. Do you like it? Good. Can I make it, please?' That's my pitching technique. (*Smooth American:*) 'Godda grade movie. This chick gets fucked and shot — ', you know. That's pitching. Selling yourself. Can't do it. Must get a 'pitch' counsellor. I had this L.A. agent for a while but she was offering me these bottom-of-the-pile, third generation, remade-15-times-before pieces of shit, hopeless dialogue ... Why do I have to put myself through this? I don't *need* this, so I've written my own script — with Adrian Deevoy — but it's not an easy script to get made ... *typically*. But it's good and my belief is that I *will* make it because I must and doing anything is only worthwhile if it's something you want to see out there. A film's gonna take a year out of your life, so it had better be something you believe in.

IDLER: At what precise point could you no longer stand your own silence?

KG: Why have I returned to music? Hm. Never stopped writing songs in my head but they went no further because, as you said, I work best collaboratively. About ten years

The Rapport by Kevin Godley from The Fun Starts Here (1981)

ago, Graham called me up. He had a melody and needed a lyric: 'Would you ─ ?' ─ 'Yeah, absolutely, come on, bring it on!' He sent me a tape but I hadn't written a lyric in a long time and created this horrible, dark thing about suicide. It wasn't quite the ticket, not really what Graham wanted so I think he got someone else to write it. He's a professional songwriter and, as such, he needs to have successful songs. As an artistic experiment, in my opinion, it was great but not targeted correctly. But we agreed to something in the future. Then a whole decade went by, and we decayed further.

IDLER: Your voice is undamaged by time. Do you still smoke?

KG: No, I quit in '95. Sue, my wife, reminded me that to direct a film you have to pass a medical, get insured, and I wasn't going to get a clean bill of health at the rate I was going.

IDLER: Were you a heavy smoker?

KG: Ooh, you know, about eighty a day. One in my mouth, one in each hand, another smouldering in the ashtray, a few more in my ears, toes, nostrils. It was a coping mechanism, being in a studio or editing suite for days on end.

IDLER: Was it easy to stop?

KG: Oh yeah. Just like that (*clicks fingers*). But that aborted song got the words coming again and I wrote 'Son Of Man' [*the backstory of pre-10cc band Hotlegs and their 1970 one-hit wonder 'Neanderthal Man'*], originally titled Rocko Doco, soon after. Our recent excursion ─ back to writing and recording ─ was to see if there was any juice left in there, anything worth making real again. What's refreshing is there's not the usual agenda, none of that 'Let's get a record deal'. So we're paying for it ourselves and doing it simply and cheaply. It's good discipline because there is a side to

me that will go on all night and day, looking for that perfect sound. Well, I've learnt over the years that that approach doesn't always work, giving yourself the widest brief possible. Sometimes less is more, it's better to narrow it, concentrate it. It's like non-linear editing in video. You can edit till the cows come home because the technology is such that you can make as many changes as you want and defer making a final decision. You're not using your head or your heart which you eventually have to do. You're not doing it solely for yourself, either, you're doing it for them to an extent. I want to get our stuff out there so other people can enjoy it, if anyone's interested. But this time no pill-sugaring.

IDLER: This is a radical approach compared to the songs you made with Lol where you would go to the studio with perhaps a sketch of a song or an idea which you would develop organically.

KG: We did both. Some songs, like 'This Sporting Life', were pre-written but we did become semi-dependent on the studio, the technology and the possibilities.

IDLER: Did you ever use those Brian Eno Oblique Strategies cards?

KG: No, we used dope. (*Laughter.*) Dope Strategies. There's only one card and you use it as a roach. The way we recorded the 'Brazilia' track on *Freeze Frame* harked back to first year art college techniques. There was this great teacher who, in order to free up your mind, would say, 'OK, I want *you* to blindfold yourself, and *you* to tie your right arm behind your back, you stand on one leg ... Now paint!' In other words, he would create obstacles for you to overcome as you did what you usually did. Painting whilst blindfolded frees you because you don't know what you are doing. What we did with Brazilia was, after we made a simple rhythm track, each of us — including Phil Manzanera — would come in independently and record something we wanted to hear. I would go in one evening to tape my vocal bits and pieces, then Lol, and then Phil, with none of us hearing what the others had done. Then we played it all back to see what happened: *'AAAARGHH! WHAAAAT?'*

IDLER: And then what? From that you recorded another, tidier version?

KG: No, the take that's on the album is it. Obviously with things that almost worked we had to slide 'em left or right a bit or clean out of sight. It's an interesting process, the element of chance.

IDLER: Has there been a mind change in your attitude to 10cc? Because in 1978 you sang on 'Group Life', 'Were we using or were we used?/'Cos on a good night when the juices flowed we cruised/But on a bad night ...' and then Lol sings a snatch of 'Donna', 10cc's first hit, suggesting that 'Donna' was a sacrifice of your artistic principles or something. Contrast that with 'Son Of Man' where you refer to 'Donna' and how 'It wrote itself in half an hour/Like all the best ones do'.

KG: I wasn't talking about Donna specifically on 'Group Life'. That song was about how something exciting can become very mundane very quickly and that's how life in 10cc was becoming after only four years.

IDLER: Stale mates.

KG: Yes, that whole treadmill scenario of come-off-tour, write-an-album, back-on-tour, write-next-album, another-tour and *(loud raspberry)*. You know, give me a fucking break. Life became a quarter-inch tape loop.

IDLER: Your last appearance as a quarter of 10cc was second on the bill to The Rolling Stones at the 1976 Knebworth Festival. What do you recall of that day?

KG: Me wearing paint spattered dungarees

and a man jumping up on stage in front of a quarter of a million people and having a wank. He did it once, was thrown off by the road crew and attempted to clamber back up for an encore but never quite made it.

The gig was awful. Everyone had to wait two hours for the sun to go down just so we could go on and show off our lovely new lights.

IDLER: How did Harvey Lisberg, the Leggy Mountbatten of the 10cc set-up, react to you and Lol's decision to quit the band at its height?

KG: Well, it was the end of the cash cow — for everybody, really — but my favourite memory of Harvey, whom I like a lot, is when he came to Strawberry Studios when Lol and I were deeply into recording Side One of *Consequences*. We played it to him and a Phonogram bigwig and they were exultant: 'Oh, fucking genius! Fantastic!' Then they went into the recording area, not knowing the mikes were open, and Harvey was like, 'Oh God help us, what the fuck was that all about???' *(Laughter)*

IDLER: Is he still your manager?

KG: What do I need a manager for? If I was actually *active* — doing loads of *stuff* — then certainly I'd need someone to pay quarter of my money to!

IDLER: You made your first stage appearance in thirty years in March when you guested at Graham's 10cc gig in Shepherds Bush.

KG: I also turned up at his Cardiff show. He asked me if I'd like to sing a song. Well, I was a bit reticent 'cos I'm not keen on nostalgia trips, but my deal was, 'I'll only sing if I can sing one of our new songs as well.' So we agreed I'd do 'Old Wild Men' from our back catalogue and 'beautifulloser.com' from GG06.

I loved it. It was an extraordinary feeling, stepping on to a stage after thirty

Avant-Garde a clue: Brass session musicians including the Clock-Watcher and the Free Jazz Timewaster.
Illustration by Kevin Godley from The Fun Starts Here *(1981)*

years. Just from a personal perspective, stepping up to a microphone and singing; the crowd went nuts —

IDLER: What, trying to get out?

KG: Yeah! 'Who's the fat guy with the white beard?'

IDLER: 'It's Howard Jacobson! He's going to give a reading!'

KG: A fantastic experience! Shepherds Bush was amazing. Just to sing live again.

IDLER: 'beautifulloser.com' is about eight minutes long. Did you remember it all?

KG: I had some prompts on the monitor but I didn't need them. I was bricking it. I didn't look at the audience, just stared into the lights. I thought I didn't move a muscle but looking at footage shot that night I was flapping and twitching like Joe Cocker on steroids.

IDLER: Although, unlike the subject of the song, you're not a woman who 'sang in the '50s, wrote songs in the '60s and acted in '75' it seems very personal to you.

KG: It is. I wrote it when I was feeling pretty low. I didn't know if there was anything creative to look forward to, if I was any good at anything, y'know, run out of steam, the end of the road ... Well, I never find it easy to write in the first person. I tend to approach songwriting like a story or screenplay. Here, the singer is telling the story of a woman who was once hugely successful and is now virtually in the gutter, in a chat room called 'beautifulloser.com'. The singer used to be one of her friends from the old days, they used to run around together, and now he's a successful businessman who owns this website and he doesn't know she's on it. So the song is about me feeling horribly sorry for myself and also betraying myself.

IDLER: In what way?

KG: Not taking the right opportunities, maybe, not pushing myself enough, being lazy. The song is about an accidental tragic betrayal. And after I'd finished writing it I stuck a shotgun in my mouth.

IDLER: 'beautifulloser.com' has suddenly become relevant in a very tragic sense when, on the 23rd of March, Kevin Whitrick hanged himself whilst on a chat room site.

KG: What's truly horrific is that people were logging on and goading him — 'Come on, go for it, get a fucking move on!' — but I suspect they thought it was a gag. They couldn't have known he was serious … Could they?

IDLER: Sly Stone sang in 1970, 'Dying young is hard to take / Selling out is harder.' That same year you, Lol and Eric Stewart were working as session musicians at Strawberry Studios — a period you once described as 'the time we sold out'. Was that hard to take?

KG: This is covered in the 'Son Of Man' song. It's the terrible struggle between Integrity and Experience. Not *that* terrible though. Yeah, we did some absolute howlers. We were finding ourselves as musicians but we weren't doing it with the luxury of Art, we just did whatever came along — TV producers' girlfriends, ventriloquists, football teams, Leslie Crowther, lunatics, you know, whoever wanted to make a record. Remember, this was in Stockport — hardly the centre of the musical universe. I dealt with it by closing down the aspirational part of my brain, getting behind the kit and playing.

IDLER: Remember 'Funky City'?

KG: The Manchester City F.C. song? Yes. (*Sings:*) 'Ci-ty … Man-ches-ter Ci-ty … '

IDLER: No, 'Funky City' was the b-side. You do a James Brown impression half-way in.

KG: Oh. Do I? 'Take me to the fridge!' Hm, yeah, we gritted our teeth and did all that shit.

IDLER: Another new song deals with physical and psychological pain and humiliation — 'Hooligan Crane'. The subject of bullying recurs in your songs —

KG: Punchbag.

IDLER: That one explicitly but it informs 'Sand In My Face', 'I Wanna Rule The World', 'The Worm And The Rattlesnake'. Years later, The Smiths weighed in with 'The Headmaster Ritual' and 'Rusholme Ruffians', their takes on the subject. Is there something rotten in Manchester schools? Were they the crappiest days of your life?

KG: Hated school. I was crap at everything and I was bullied — what else is there?

IDLER: Why you, though? It was the beard, wasn't it?

KG: They didn't just pick on me, they picked on fucking everybody! It wasn't a one-man show. But, long after, I bumped into one of them. I'd been quite successful by then and was standing outside a car showroom in Manchester, looking at an AC428 Fastback, when I was tapped on the shoulder by an eight foot tall policeman who used to be one of the school bullies.

IDLER: Did he beat you up for old times' sake?

KG: No, he was very sweet actually but I couldn't help thinking, 'You're a policeman, I'm a rock star. The meek shall inherit the earth.'

I was at the North Cestrian Grammar School in Altrincham and the school motto was '*Delapsus resurgam*' — 'When I fall I

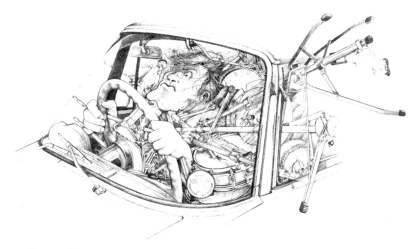

A quiff and a spliff and a drums overdose, KG's teen tub-thumper chases the rock 'n' roll dream. From 'The Fun Starts Here'.

shall rise' — which I refer to obliquely in 'Hooligan Crane': 'It's written on the tie'. Being bullied is so traumatic. I had to get the train home every day and I was stripped by them on it. They tore my clothes off and threw them down the corridor. That's a horrible thing to do to anyone.

You daren't use the school toilets. It was all right to have a pee but you couldn't have a shit. But I needed to have a shit so I went in the cubicle, sat there, and then all these faces appeared above my head. (*Chants:*) 'You're having a shi-it!' (*Fight noises.*) TSS. Traumatic Shit Syndrome.

I always had the impression that other kids were laughing at me and I think I became the person I am now to counteract these feelings of inadequacy. If people are going to look at me, let it be for something good.

IDLER: The bullying wasn't purely down to anti-Semitism? Punchbag mentions '"Dirty Jew" was written on the blackboard' and 'Your Christian soldiers smell blood'.

KG: Jews are traditionally the underdog — particularly when there are only three in the school. But how I eventually escaped being a target was by drawing pictures of nude women and selling them for sixpence. That's pretty Jew-*ish*, don't you think? It was also my grand entrance into the worlds of art and commerce. Of course, at that age I hadn't a clue as to what was going on under ladies' garments — neither did my customers, luckily. I couldn't imagine what a woman's front bottom looked like so, by not drawing anything, I was almost right by default. The tits probably had no nipples on them, but it satisfied a certain craving or curiosity. I did a rip-roaring trade, peddling my studies of nipple-less women. Think I'll release a limited edition of nipples for lucky collectors.

IDLER: I'm not denigrating or demeaning your output with Lol, but what moves me in yours and Graham's new songs is the directness. There's none of the loopy deviations of your past songs, they cut to the

The band that fashion forgot

quick. Do you think that's down to an awareness of mortality, a sense of time growing shorter and 'I can't fuck around now; this is what I need to say'?

KG: That's partially it. Having been a writer, sporadically, for a long time, I've written in lots of styles. It can be so easy to write impressionistic lyrics that are merely part of the overall sound. But, right now, I don't want that. I want to be extremely clear about what I'm saying, which is why on the website each song has a short synopsis of what it's about. There's none of that 'It can mean whatever you want it to mean' thing. That attitude is fine and certain people do it exceedingly well. The Beatles did it well; they wrote about fuck all sometimes. Bowie does it bloody well. but it doesn't work for me now. It's more about, 'Have I said what i wanted to say? No. Try again. Have I said it now? Yes. Good. Next!'

IDLER: Is it true you sang backing vocals on The Clash's 'Bankrobber'?

KG: What? Dunno. I was in the studio with them up in Manchester when they did it. Yes, with Mikey Dread. Good question. It's possible. (*Hums the riff.*) I was just following the spliff. I liked The Clash a lot. Seen them a couple of times. Sorry, memory's a blurrrrrr ... I recall Sue and I watching them from the side of a stage and Mick Jones came over and gobbed on the floor as a greeting. Marvellous!

IDLER: It was weird, that Year Zero stance that Punk had about wiping out the rock dinosaurs. An early interview with the Pistols was in a pub and Steve Jones was all, 'Get rid of these boring old farts, this old irrelevant rubbish!' Then 'I'm Mandy, Fly Me' came on the jukebox and Jones exclaimed, 'Ah! Love the guitar on this!'

KG: Things are never as black and white as the media like to paint it. There's lots of grey areas — like John Lydon being a Kate Bush fan.

IDLER: Randy Newman wrote a cameo called 'Interiors' which begins with him admitting that he can't say what he feels and that 'everything becomes a joke', whereupon he tells a joke and ends the song by apologising. I thought that was an acute show of man's self-consciousness in openly declaring their deepest feelings, for fear of appearing vulnerable, maudlin, needy and weedy. It wasn't really until your final album with Lol, *Goodbye Blue Sky*, that you addressed themes of love and devotion in a non-flippant fashion. Those songs — 'Golden Rings', 'Sweet Memory' and 'Hidden Heartbeat' — were a breakthrough, and your new songs with Graham, 'The Same Road' and 'Johnny Hurts', continue the development. Are you comfortable without the jester's cap and bells?

KG: Big time. I never was truly comfortable with the humour tag. Humour in song doesn't sit well with me anymore. 'Hospital Song', 'I Wanna Rule The World'— great in their time. I can't be funny in music anymore. I can do wry, I can do dry, can't do funny.

IDLER: That's another difference between Lol and yourself. Lol's song 'Life Is A Minestrone' is soup-to-nuts punnery— 'The seat of learning and the flush of success relieves a constipated mind'.

KG: It's bright and it's fun and it's exceedingly well done but, now I'm writing for now, that style of lyric isn't my thing. It's not real. It's not how the world is, either.

IDLER: What was the first illicit substance you tried?

KG: Marijuana. Art school time. A lady friend went to Moss Side to score our first joint for us. We took it back to college, too scared to try it for three days—hid it in a damp drawer—finally plucked up the courage to smoke it. The air went wavy and I puked. I said, 'I don't like *this* . . . Better try it again.' (*Laughs*)

Hashish was my drug of choice. Did coke for a couple of years—the '80s, you know? I hated cocaine in the end: we were doing really long nights, editing in New York, and that was the drug of the day. Had hash cake once, disastrously. Had seven pieces, not knowing. Halluci-nated for three days during a video recce in LA. And I snorted heroin once.

IDLER: What did you think of that?

KG: Fucking brilliant! Which is why I never did it again. I had it by accident, thinking it was not-nice-coloured cocaine. It was quite extraordinary. It gets rid of the anxious black knot in your stomach everyone has, just dissolves it away. I can see how getting addicted is so easy.

IDLER: What about sulphate?

KG: Lol and I were in the studio, dopeless for once, but there was some speed so we had that and cut this chugging blues song. We were convinced it was pure genius, a solid gold rock classic. We played it back the next day to discover it was absolute garbage, the worst thing we had ever done. It's the only song of ours I think that remains unreleased.

IDLER: Now that you're a non-smoker, do you support the government's total ban on smoking?

KG: Fuck 'em. If there must be a *law* against it in public places there should be a place to go where smoking is compulsory. If you don't like smoke and everyone's smoking, go somewhere else. If you want to smoke but nobody else is smoking, go somewhere else. The anti-everything fascists are taking over the world.

IDLER: What about the health fascists? Supermarket products have stickers advising you to eat five pieces of fruit a day.

KG: Or what? I'm going to get arrested if I eat *six*—or only four? It's a *law*, is it? Oh fuck, the world is turning to shit and they are attempting to correct it with fruit intake. The world will be fine if we all eat five pieces of fruit a day? We're all gonna be gone in a hundred years so, please, let's just get on with it.

Blanche d'Arcount by Lindsay Brunnock

ESSAYS

I'M NOT MAD ABOUT IT

GWYN

THE RISE OF

FRANTIC SEX

AND HOW TO RESIST IT

by Michael Bywater

HE TROUBLE WITH LUNATICS IS NOT THAT THEY'RE MAD. WE'RE
all mad. Take the top off anyone's head and you'll find a seething Babel of
delusions, usually glamourised under such headings as Hopes, Dreams,
Ambitions, Thoughts, Religious Beliefs and Me. 'Me' is the biggest delusion of them
all: a squirt of protoplasm, a handful of happenstance, a brief venerean urge and
here we are, making a fuss. We're all mad.

But the trouble with lunatics is that they're *frantic*. And somehow they're
running the asylum now. *Frantic* is the chief characteristic of 21st century life.
Frantic drivers, frantic hamburger joints, frantic industry (what could be more
frantic than the 'just-in-time' production theory?), frantic businessmen employing
frantic accountants to frantically maximise money, which will be expended on frantic pursuits. All that snowboarding and eco-tourism, the multi-function watches,
the in-car GPS, the Blackberrys, the downloads; FaceBook, Google, Nike, Airbus,
Fast Track, check-in, upgrade, ready-to-wear Second Life no-waiting low choles-
terol worked-out multiply-orgasmic toned tanned six-packed fate-of-the-earth
wash-'n'-go portfolio-career'd Brand *Me* logo-stamped over-achieving Gehenna:
frantic, frantic, frantic. We have taken our cue from the lunatics, and are the worse
off for it.

The frantic now have an entire culture — the dominant culture — devoted to
them. Frantic music is presented by frantic DJs; films slice and dice in cuts of *no more
than two seconds*, the odd homogeneous culture of our cities (the soothing snarl and
rumble of London, the soporific rattle of a train) has *frantic* overlaid upon it by the
inevitable iPod or bleeping mobile. There are even frantic news-papers, most
notably the *Daily Mail* and the *Sunday Times*, the former being the equivalent of
the Department of Homeland Security (not there to keep us safe but to keep us
frightened) and the latter there to let us know that, while we may *think* we're doing

okay, there are people with much more money having more glamorous exciting *interesting* sex with more famous, thinner people in bigger, posher houses under bluer, more exclusive skies which they reached in faster cars along emptier roads than we will ever experience unless we get *more frantic*.

Sometimes this is called 'youth culture' but that's unfair. The young may often *appear* frantic; but that's because (a) they don't really know what's going on, (b) are afflicted with an excess of animal spirits and (c) are engaged in the ineluctable mating-dance of Nature. Good for them.

The *real* frantic are much more likely to be middle-aged, driven by the sense that time is running out and desperate to buy, or otherwise acquire, some respite. Foolish. If time's ever-rolling stream bears us all away, the sensible thing to do is put on a bit of weight (fat floats) then lie back in the lifejacket position and go with the flow. But where's the money in that? Who — if everyone is floating — has got the upper hand?

And so we inhabit the Petticoat Lane paradigm of life. Our umbrellas are stolen at one end of the street and then sold back to us at the other. It is no longer permissible to wear that ancient tweed coat that has been through so much with us; instead, we must buy a new one, carefully constructed to look like one we've had for ever. In the Frantic World, we're all *arrivistes*. Process is substituted for outcome. In the morning I shave with a badger brush* and some shaving soap (I used to use Trumper's Violet but they've gone Frantic now so it's Mitchell's Wool Fat Soap for me, and you'd do well to follow my example) and a double-edged safety razor with blades costing eightpence a piece. This is not the Frantic way. The Frantic way says I should use a Gillette Fusion which, for God's sake, *vibrates* and looks like an athletic shoe and has *six blades*; and with this, I should use a special shaving gloop which looks and smells like engine-grease and has, as far as I can understand it, magnetic balls† in it; and so a pleasantly contemplative beginning to the day — the hot flannel, the whipping up of a fine lather on the face, the careful stroke of steel on chin, the Moss Scuttle to keep the lather warm, the unequivocal reminder that one is a *man*, not a foolish metrosexual — is replaced by a Frantic buzzing of 'technology' and ugliness and the smell of chemicals and, at the end of it, a *far worse shave* followed by ingrown hairs and razor-burn.

---

* I'll have to get a licence for it soon, as they're doing with Scotsmen's sporrans, to prove it wasn't improperly killed, or alternatively was Chinese, because the animal welfare people don't care about Chinese badgers.

† Some sort of balls, anyway.

And why? So that I can become the simulacrum of myself which has been shown to me on television: a modern, Frantic 'man', foolish enough to spend £2.50 on a sodding *razor blade*. And instead of the pleasant rosewater soothing of D R Harris's Pink After-Shave Lotion, it must be some abominable Frantic 'cologne' bought because it is advertised by a picture of a Muscle Mary in a boat in a creek.

But worst of all is the rise of Frantic Sex.

Once again, the mechanism is the same: the Petticoat Lane Paradigm, this time run by the pornography industry. The pornographers stole real sex and made it Frantic. Frantic women with frantic improbable breasts, thrashing about as if tossed in a lifeboat in a force ten gale. They hurtle into Frantic orgasms at the sight of a man, half-blind on Viagra, fiddling with himself; they squeal and shout and sigh, though most of us, confronted by a woman making such a racket in our own beds, would immediately desist and (according to our dispositions) chuck her out or speak soothingly and call a doctor. They change positions constantly, like a man trying to get to sleep on a train, or pound away frantically as if trying (but failing) to get it over with.

And this is what the poor readers of the *Sunday Times* believe 'celebrities' and Russian oligarchs with their bought-and-paid-for silicone wives — or even, God help us, Rod Stewart — are getting, and come to believe that *they want it too*.

They do not. I speak with the authority of a breadth of experience which would make you want to kill me from envy if you knew the half of it; but *they do not*. That sort of sex is the equivalent of some diabolical combination of fast food and the over-laid-up emptiness of those restaurants which you always feel are run as a tax shelter by Syrian gynaecologists, and the other customers are all arms dealers. It is the carnal equivalent of the Gillette Fusion: a lot of fuss and nothing to show for it.

I'm not saying this because I'm past it; just no longer Frantic. In the *Symposium*, Plato has an imaginary Aristophanes quizzed whether it's true he can't get it up any more, and if it bothers him. Not a bit, says Aristophanes (one of the original masters, in life, of the knob joke); the expiry of sexual desire is like being unchained from a madman.‡ And yet now, thanks to technology, we have Viagra, which is no more than the hydraulic equivalent of those extensible dog-leads: a way of reeling the madman back into propinquity so that one may deliver an

---

‡ A scene I always imagine, for some reason, to be taking place on Clapham Common, in a light drizzle, at dusk, the madman stark naked and capering away into the distance, gibbering incoherently, like a baboon.

imitation — even in the absence of desire or native capability — of the men (poor wooden simulacra) in the pornographic films, and hopefully with a woman thrashing and scratching and shifting about and screaming 'Yes yes yes!' when what she really means is 'Dear Lord in heaven let him stop.'

It is a terrible prospect, Frantic Sex, and the antithesis of the real thing, which might be called 'Idle Sex' except it so often it never gets to the sex bit. Idle Languor might be more accurate; Idle Sex would be too close to that terrible Tantric nonsense, with the silly Lingam Dance (wily-waggling, like the madman in the drizzle) and Yoni Worship ('Yes, very nice, dear, who'd have thought it?') and the abominable Plumber's Position (so called because you stay in for hours but nobody comes). Idle Languor may end in a volcanic finale which leaves both (or all) involved beached and startled; but it is equally likely to end with the word 'volcanic' crossing the mind of one of the parties who is then reminded of the death of Pliny the Elder in the Vesuvian eruption of 79AD, and who says so, and — this *never* happens in Frantic Sex, just as nobody ever laughs — leads into a conversation about volcanoes, or Naples, or historiography, or what the Romans ate for dinner, or anything you like.

Idle Languor, in short, is not goal-directed, and you only have to look at the great erotic paintings of the past to see that it, not Frantic Sex, was once the great *desideratum*. Can you imagine Manet's *Olympia* thrashing and squealing? No. What would she have done, had you been able to afford her? *Nothing*. She would have possessed that greatest of all erotic skills: inertia. Inertia coupled with a limitless hospitality of the body. Even that enemy of the carnal, Evelyn Waugh, knew as much when his narrator in *Brideshead Revisited* spoke of his woman as an estate which he would enter upon and explore at his leisure: here a glade, there a park; lakes, hedges, coppices, a rose-garden, a *grande pelouse* and nobody shrieking or wriggling or, in that frightful Germanic way that has become so popular§ with its swings and harnesses and electrodes and buzzers. All that effort. All that *noise*.

The late Julie Burchill¶ once wrote a telling scene in a novel of the Eighties, now fallen into obscurity, in which she described her heroine's thoughts when, her career falling about her ears, her husband began slowly creeping down beneath the duvet. *Oh God* she thought (I paraphrase from memory) *as if she didn't have enough on her plate, now Matthew had to choose this moment to be Good In Bed.*

---

§ Germans, of course, being unable to enjoy anything unless it involves rules, a catalogue, and a certain capital outlay.

¶ I don't know why I think of her as being 'late' since she is still alive, but you know what I mean.

There is, in Idle Languor, no room for *Good In Bed*. It is not only permissible to fall asleep afterwards, but before and indeed during. The proceedings may be interrupted for, or substituted by, a cup of tea. In the old days when the government let us smoke, there could have been not just the post-coital cigarette, but a cigarette break in the middle. Or, indeed, a cigarette *instead*. Idle Languor has nothing particularly in mind; it is more conversation than conquest, and will drift where it may. It is, in short, the opposite of, and a perfect antidote to, the tyranny of the Frantic, and I would commend it to you more persuasively except I find myself slowly... f

a

/

/

i

n

g

∴

a

s

—

⋮

WHAT IT IS TO BE A PERSON.

LORDS OF MISRULE

The true spirit of Christmas is rude, raucous,
drunken and noisy, says Jay Griffiths.

Illustrated by Alice Smith

SINGING AS HE VOMITS DOWN HIS TROUSERS, THE BLOKE IN THE
reindeer-horn hat is surrounded by a cheering crowd of pissheads, twirling,
from his point of view, around the lamppost he is clinging to. No one sober
appreciates him; the bourgeoisie think he's vulgar, the police say he is disturbing the
peace, the Church thinks he dishonours the spirit of crimble, the government tuts
about binge drinking, the media attack him as a buffoon and moan about the decline
of moral values. A fool, an ass, a clown, joker and dickhead: actually he is the ves-
tige of something ancient, a perky manifestation of a profound figure in our culture,
part of the earthiness of all festival.

Festival has a tatterdemalion democracy, common as muck. The midwinter
carnival is a grassroots affair, which, incidentally, is why all tasteful Christmas
decorations look so misplaced. The spirit of Christmas is not restrained or well-
heeled, but excessive and vulgar in its original sense: of the common people.
The natural emblems of Christmas are always the common or garden leaves, the
seasonal holly and ivy which you pick for free, not the pampered horticulture of
expensive flowers bought out of season.

Carnival is political to the core; throwing its knickers at the bourgeoisie, over-
throwing the status quo. Anti-hierarchical and anti-aristocratic, its deepest roots
involve the commoners behaving badly, which is exactly why the person who best
honours the spirit of Christmas is not the sober parishioner on their knees praying
for the Queen at ten thirty in the morning, but the bloke outside the pub with his
ludicrous Rudolf hat. Revellers are levellers all, in a spirited, unbounded hulla-
baloo let loose till the rulers are nervous. Revellers are rebellious, inherently and
indeed linguistically, for the Old French word 'revel' means rebellion, tumult, disturbance and noisy mirth. The Queen can get stuffed, and the horny god in his
Rudolf manifestation would be only too happy to oblige.

Though he may not know it, the bloke in the reindeer hat suggests a long
history which can be glimpsed in the medieval characters, the Lord of Misrule,

the Abbot of Unreason, the King of the Bean and Pope of Fools: these were the people in charge — if that is the term — of Christmas revels. Chosen by lottery, the Lord of Misrule presided over the Feast of Fools, 'an ebullition of the natural lout beneath the cassock' according to historian E K Chambers. Celebrated by the lower clergy, this was a nut-cracking, topsy-turvy homage to reversal; mocking their superiors, a Mock King was one of the titles of the season. Men dressed as women, choirboys were robed in papal attire, and a Boy Bishop was appointed: a burlesque, bottoms-up and pants-down piss-take of the Bishoprick, it really was taking the episcopal. Riotous and rude, singing lewd songs in church, eating black pudding at the altar during mass, the lower orders wore bawdy masks and disguises, played dice, recited scurrilous verses and made indecent gestures (presumably with the black pudding).

The roots of it go back to the Roman midwinter Saturnalia, in honour of the god of seed. A slave was chosen as lord of the revels, and the normal hierarchies of power were reversed so masters would wait on servants. This festival, says Lucian, was marked by 'drinking and being drunk, noise and games and dice ... feasting of slaves, singing naked.' Licence is a crucial strand in all festival; licentious behaviour and things permitted in the festive season which are not otherwise sanctioned, though it can be argued that carnival in fact supports the status quo because it offers a short and limited licence allowing people to let off steam without effecting permanent change.

Another influence was the Kalends, linked to the winter festival of Dionysus, which featured masquerades including people wearing animal hides or the heads of beasts, antlers and horns. Dionysus, the horny god, earthiest of them all, associated with boozing, excess, sexual licence and non-rational forces, was god of wildness and having a wild time. Dionysiac revels included a horn or phallus too large for one person to hold, and the god was accompanied by the 'Komos', the ancient version of the crowd of pissheads around the lamppost, and their song was the 'Komoidia' from where the word 'comedy' comes.

Carnival overturns not only the usual hierarchies of society but also the usual hierarchies of thought, so, in the medieval Christmas, Mockery was crowned king, and Subservience could sod off. Unreason was applauded and given its own Abbot, while Logic and Reason went down the pan. Misrule was lauded and lorded, while Order could stew in its own juice.

The bloke in the reindeer hat wipes his mouth on an old lottery ticket. At the Feast of Fools, the junior clergy gambled, played cards and used dice. Dice? Gambling? Cards? Choosing the Lord of Misrule by lottery? Enter one of the Church's most hated abstract nouns: Chance. Anarchic and devilish, chance was the enemy of order, of god's predestined will, the whirligig roulette of luck set against the rigid linearity of Judaeo-Christian time. Chance was also important in the political analysis which these festivities yielded, for they revealed the essentially arbitrary quality of social hierarchy, the accident of birth which makes one Mrs. Windsor a queen, and another a part-time assistant at the Bingo hall in Streatham. No wonder today's middle classes disdain the lottery. Luck is vulgar.

If the junior clergy played at cards, chanciest of all the cards is the jester who overturns all the rules, taking precedence over the King and Queen. The jester is an enigmatic figure; often masked, carrying his rude jester stick with balls and bells, wearing furs and feathers, associated with nature. Who is he? A portmanteau man, he is the Fool, the Clown, the Wild Man, — a kind of lifelong Lord of Misrule. In Central Europe, at Christmas, masquerading troupes run wild, headed by a 'wild man' or 'fool' — exactly the same is true in Soho or central Manchester for the Wild Man has many guises and he plays through many players, especially at Christmas.

The Fool is profoundly associated with shamanism, for example the magnetic Feste the jester in Shakespeare's *Twelfth Night* entering with his pipe and drum, is as certain a shaman as any Siberian robed in bearskin, beating his drum. This is where the ancient and important figure of the clown parts company with the bloke in the reindeer hat. For the shaman's primary role was to be eloquent of nature, to know its seasons, to understand animals, to heal with natural plants. Today, in a culture which has temporarily mislaid its shamanism, the joker falls flat on his face, and the clown is just that. Part of the shamanic role is shapeshifting, dressing as an animal or bird, playing out the wildness within; from this tradition come the Dionysiac revels and Christmas masques and mummers. Any shaman would understand the shapeshifting aspect of wearing reindeer horns, but the bloke clutching the lamppost has no idea. How could he? Urban modernity is too distanced from nature, living at one remove from seasonal time and earth knowledge. The jester without the vision, wit without wisdom, the relics of the costume without the function of it, the quotation without the translation.

The medieval Feast of Fools was the festival of the lower clergy. The higher orders hated it. They could smell the shaman behind the fool; they sniffed the devilry of chance; the whole affair reeked of pagan earthiness, and far too much fun. They repeatedly and unsuccessfully tried to prohibit it, so it was outlawed by the Church in the fifteenth century, and suppressed by Queen Mary in the sixteenth. The Puritans tried to ban the whole idea of midwinter frolics, best illustrated in the battle between Feste and the Puritan Malvolio, wanting to forbid Sir Toby Belch his cakes and ale.

Of all the authorities, the crossest of the lot was Bishop Robert Grosseteste, a name to conjure with, especially if you're a pissed-off member of the junior clergy. There was no one more determined to suppress the bawdiness of the Feast of Fools. But then, perhaps, there was no one so spurred to do it by having a name so given to alliterative piss-taking as Bishop Bob Big-Balls. (And what if he wasn't well hung?)

But the Church was up against something it has never, ever defeated. It was up against the essential comedy of life, lusty, funny, rude and sexual, the cock of it all, the cunt of the thing, the robust wink of the jester just fiddling with his balls. (Calm down, madam.) No matter how much a Bishop might get his knickers in a twist, no matter how grey and repressive the Church's orders, there has always been rude rebellion in the ranks, and revelry running underground. The spirit of midwinter glee bubbles up, belching and farting, hiccuping, trumpeting, giggly with fizzy booze, and exuberantly opposed to the liturgical groans of the Church.

'If music be the food of love, play on, give me excess' are the first twelve words of *Twelfth Night*, and the lines are effortlessly eloquent of the comedy of life: music, food, love, play, gifts and excess. The hunger for these things is an unappeasable, sensual, human longing for the feast. The word feast is linked to festival, fiesta, festoon and indeed to Feste. Feasting is glorious excess, the just-say-yes to life, to the huge plum pudding and too many sausages, to the bucketful of wine and the six-cheese sauce, to the extra mince pies and too much brandy butter, the seconds of chestnut stuffing, to more, more, more.

This authentic appetite for life is healthy and vibrant; the urge to bite the apple, to suck the juices, to relish the cakes and ale. But it is perverted by modernity into merely material consumption, characterized by control — the dictates of the fashion industry or the power of advertising; consumption whose most salient quality is the purchase not the enjoyment. Authentic appetite is also mediated by modernity, rather than being directly experienced; a longing to clown around at midnight is perverted into blearily watching some telly celebrity doing the clowning for you. The exhaustive consumption of a shopping trip rather than energetic appetite for the feast which is the rule of comedy.

Comedy is far truer to the nature of life than tragedy is. Life survives through the effervescence of comedy not the oppressiveness of tragedy. Comedy is set among the common people while tragedy is set in the courts, with the lords and dignitaries. Comedy is gregarious and is inherently, gorgeously, promiscuous: have another one, another fuck, another feast. Tragedy is enclosed indoors, as far from nature as possible. Comedy takes place outdoors, within nature. The comedy of nature and the nature of comedy is feral, wild, tough and played out in the midwinter drama: spring will wrestle with winter and will win every time.

The bloke with the reindeer hat lurches back into the pub to nick the mistletoe and dangles it over his horns. He is a chancer. 'Fancy a shag?' he gurgles at a passer-by as he re-sees his kebab. Sex is at the very heart of festival. The Saturnalia was held to encourage seed growth and the fertility of vegetation. Mistletoe, traditional mid-winter plant, was thought to represent fertility, its spurt of white seed a semen arc. Look again at chubby, ruby-nosed Santa, a gnomic little figure, tumescent and always about to burst at the seams, his white beard frothing over his cheeks, and, grinning with his sacks bulging, see how he comes, squeezing himself down tight chimneys and looking for dark, damp nooks, watch how lovingly he approaches the single stocking, warm, soft, waiting at midnight, which he stuffs with his goodies and fills with his nuts.

The Feast of Fools was also known as the Feast of Asses, celebrating not God in the highest, but the lowest of creatures, reversing significance. The ass is a pagan symbol of fertility and strength, and at the same time the epitome of stupidity. Taking a cue from the Abbot of Unreason, the ass suggests the most unreasoning part of us, our sexual selves. (We do not, cannot, choose who we want to fuck.) The ass is our animal nature, irrational, the animal which we all shapeshift into when we make love, away from reason and the clock, away from the orderly world. Sex itself is the ultimate Lord of Misrule, the lusty Dionysus in us all. The reindeer is a horny beast and the Feast of Asses featured a 'bald-headed, red-nosed clown.' 'Nuff said.

The Feast of Fools was most celebrated on January 1st, the official Feast of Circumcision. The Church wanted to celebrate the pruning of Christ's bits; and with exquisite appropriateness, the lower orders, who were often treated as a bit of a rude nuisance by the Church (the natural lout playing with himself under the cassock) chose this as their particular feast day.

In the body of Christ the members of the lower orders were the groin, that member so given to uprisings against the authorities at the head. No wonder the Church authorities wanted to cut the festival down to size. No wonder they never could. No wonder the modern-day Puritans want to suppress the vulgar excesses of festivity and no wonder they never can. You can't keep this spirit down, for it rises again, of its own sweet will. Every morning, every night, and quite often in between, *ping!* he is risen. As common, as natural, as earthy, as irrational, as carnivalesque, as festive, as comedic, as playful, as jesterish, wild and anarchic as the rebellious revelry of Christmas with its gleeful, cocky risorgimento for effervescent life. Cheers.

William Hogarth (1697–1764): 'Before'
cica 1730–31, oil on canvas, 365mm x 448mm
Fitzwilliam Museum, University of Cambridge

William Hogarth (1697–1764): 'After'
cica 1730–31, oil on canvas, 370mm x 446mm
Fitzwilliam Museum, University of Cambridge

OFF THE JOB

Didn't sex used to be fun,
asks Nick Lezard

SEX, I HAVE COME TO UNDERSTAND, IS NOT FUN. THERE. I'VE said it. You find it hard to believe? I can't blame you. It is a counter-intuitive proposition, to say the least. Sex has got to be fun, hasn't it? Otherwise we wouldn't think about it so much. The primal pleasurable feeling is, after and before all, the stimulation of the genitals. Even the prepubescent know this. Especially the prepubescent. That's what Freud worked out, to the alarm and consternation of the remnants of the Victorians, who had spent a good deal of the previous decades idealising and sentimentalising the innocence of children.

But that's not the end of the matter. There's more to fun than just pleasure, and more to pleasure than just fun.

You will find no better illustration of the complicated relation between sex and fun in the diptych painted by Hogarth called *Before* and *After*. Look at the man's almost horrified expression; compare it with his sleazy *savoir-faire* in *Before*. Like-wise compare the woman's coyness in *Before* with the odd mixture of wantonness and need she displays in *After*. The postures Hogarth gives his protagonists is perfect, absolutely and immediately familiar to us centuries on. The pair have obviously undergone a cataclysmic event, one quite at odds with the studied formality that has been used to achieve it. The preceding picture is all artifice: the man's practised charm, the woman's equally practised modesty, are the poses expected of them in order for them to achieve their ends. The man has to be the smooth seducer, the woman has to make a token show of resistance, let the man know that what she has to offer will not be given up without a struggle — an unreal struggle, that is. (Surrendering one's virtue after a real struggle means you have been raped; and indeed Hogarth made other representations of *Before* and *After* where it appears that a rape is precisely what has taken place. There are those who say that all male/female sexual acts are acts of rape, but I am not one of them, so treat the experience as, thankfully, aberrant, and leave the uglier side male desire to others. Still, Hogarth may have been ambivalent at times in his portrayal of women — in his *Satan, Sin and Death*, Sin is represented as a bare-breasted woman, but here he pinpointed the problematic nature of male desire.)

In *After*, their gazes do not quite meet each other; but it is clear that the man is more traumatised than the woman, both literally and figuratively undone, his bare genitals a taunt to whatever decorum he may have been displaying before. She, though also indecently exposed, has a tenderer, more needy expression her face. She wants the man to hang around, say something nice, make some expression or gesture of tenderness and commitment; he just wants to get the fuck out of there. So to speak.

Men, do not protest. This is how you feel after most casual sexual encounters. After an inappropriate sexual encounter, such as involves adultery or the seedier end of prostitution, you feel it squared, and it makes no difference how much energy, ingenuity or cash you have used in order to have that sexual encounter in the first place. *Post coitum omnes animal tristes est*, but it is still a compulsion to have the coitus in the first place. Look at poor Thermos O'Flask, condemned in the pages of *Viz* to surrender to his craving for cheap prostitutes. In one strip he is tossed off by a slag behind a rubbish skip; on coming into money, he now has the same prostitute do the same thing to him, except that she is wearing a mink coat and the skip is full of diamonds. In other words, no amount of money thrown at the situation can eradicate the sense of shame experienced at the whole transaction. In fact, the shame is the point.

As if sex were not already not fun enough, I notice my twelve-year-old daughter's homework from her PHSE class. (I have to ask what the acronym stands for: Personal Health and Social education, apparently, although what that 'social' means is not something I am quite sure of.) It comes in the form of a very primitive crossword, with 40-odd clues. For someone like myself, whose sex education was limited to a brief, embarrassed digression from pistils and stamens to the, um, penis and um, vagina, this assignment comes as something of a shock. One down: 'type of hair in intimate areas (5)'. Easy: 'pubic'. My daughter, who, the last time I looked (a couple of years ago), had none, gets that. Jesus, I remember what happened to a classmate during Latin when he wittily renamed the Punic Wars the Pubic Wars. And another who murmured 'scrotum' when we were informed that the Latin for a shield was *scutum*. They were actually beaten. This in a school where corporal punishment was only nominally on the books, reserved for crimes like arson or murdering the physics teacher. Now twelve-year-olds, at a school which is highly religious, are being obliged to write down words whose utterance or inscription would, in my day, have resulted in either a thrashing, a visit to the headmaster, an awkward conference with my parents, or most likely all three. 'Wet dream.' 'Erection.' 'Sperm.' 'Masturbate.' ('To touch self for pleasure.') These are the words she knows. Along with ones which attest to a more problematic, adult world of sexuality. 'Consent'. 'Condom'. 'Divorce'. Many of the ones she doesn't get, I can't get either. What the hell is a thirteen-letter word, beginning with S and ending O_E_, meaning 'external sanitation'? Or its internal equivalent, beginning with T and ending O_ (6)? I can complete the Guardian's cryptic crossword occasionally, but I'm stumped here. (Actually, I work it out a couple of days later. 'Tampon'. I think.)

My wife, and, indeed, my daughter, both find it hilarious that I am so bothered by this assignment, and others like it. I am teased horribly by them. Looked at objectively, and with my libertarian glasses on, the exercise is wholly sensible and enlightened. But I can't help thinking that part of the fun I had in growing up and discovering sex was that it was murky. One had to go to some lengths to shed light on the matter. At school, a clandestine copy of The Little Red Book, a subversive volume which contained such otherwise forbidden information, was circulated with the same feeling of danger and excitement that a samizdat copy of Nineteen Eighty-Four would have generated in Soviet-era Russia. Personally, I do not think I have suffered. It may have taken me an unbelievably long time to be disabused of the notion that women did not ejaculate eggs when they orgasmed, but I never got anyone pregnant or suffered any confusion as to what to stick in where. The main problem, as I vividly remember it, was whether I was ever going to have any sex in the first place. Knowing the definition of 'discharging undeveloped baby (11)' was some considerable way, when I was twelve, from what I would have considered to be useful information. True, my daughter is at a girls' school, and many of her class-mates are rather more physically developed than she is. This kind of thing is useful. But I am interested by the way the lesson has been imparted: in what is normally considered a recreational form. It is as if an acknowledgment is being made that all the fun is being drained out of sex, and of learning about sex; only the trace-element of fun, in the form of a word puzzle, remains. And it is symptomatic of a kind of heavy-handed, po-faced, joyless earnestness which extends itself right the way through society, in areas which have nothing to do with sex. I hesitate to use the phrase 'nanny state', but there is something nightmarishly nannyish about this: not the nanny who disapprovingly raps a boy's erection with a cold teaspoon, but one who, upon noticing an erection, goes through all its physical causes and effects. Which to my primitive mind, is even worse. Where's the fun in that? And what will be the effects on this, the first generation in the history of humanity to be subjected to this kind of detailed education? No wonder the young are retreating to virtual worlds where the only kind of sexual contact is imaginary.

So whatever happened to the idea of sex as fun? It doesn't actually exist as an artistic possibility any more, which is surprising, considering the 1960s were meant

to blow this kind of fuddy-duddiness away for good. You can see why sex, in the
18th- and 19th-century novel, is, unless it takes place offstage and is meant to
produce babies for married couples, a disaster; you can see why Evelyn Waugh, in
A Handful of Dust, called extra-marital sex 'base love'; but it takes a brave and rare
artist now, even now, to say that sex with whoever you like is fun. I can think of
a strip by the comic artist Steve Bell, declaring that sex should be a 'deeply fun'
activity ('boing, boing', go the bedsprings; he has also, in another of his *Guardian*
'If...' strips, declared for the beneficial effects of masturbation); but that's really
about it. Even in farce, comic, fun sex is simply sex waiting for a comeuppance. It
seems that the last truly sexually liberated age in this country at least was in the
Restoration; with pockets of it surviving into the age of Boswell. And, indeed, the
immediate proximity of Boswell, that is, whoever happened to be stuck on the end
of Boswell's dick (i.e. Boswell, not necessarily the unfortunate jade he
happened to be poking). What is it now? Something to be studied when a child;
encouraged, in an antiseptic, therapeutic way, in the problem pages of newspapers. Or if not antiseptic and therapeutic, then still somehow revolting, as if a pair
of ramblers were talking about a naughty but invigorating walk in the Cheviots.

THE CONSOLATIONS OF PORNOGRAPHY

❖

PORNOGRAPHY purports to be, or proclaims itself to be, sex as fun, as
nothing but fun, irresponsible, ecstatic, shorn of consequences. This may
not be true of its wilder outreaches, or what it can look like when one
contemplates the grunting, mulletted, mustachioed German of popular iconography, and indeed not at all if one follows the plausible feminist argument about
exploitation — but that's what it says it's all about. It's also about more than that,
of course. The graphic representation of intercourse has been going on for pretty
much as long as graphic representation of anything. It's more than just a contract
between the pornographer and the reader, delivering sex as solitaire, one that
always comes out; it stirs the primal urges in a way that one knows, instinctively,
is deliciously wrong. There are plenty of people who are tuned in enough to this
sense of wrongness to find all pornography, and the very idea of pornography,
disgusting; but there are enough of the other kind of people to make pornography
the most thriving business on the planet. The internet, which allows people to feast

their eyeballs on as much of the stuff as they can take without the old-fashioned embarrassment of having to buy the stuff from a newsagent or enter, shoulders hunched in shame, a sex shop devoted to the stuff (that would always take an enormous effort of will on my part, unless deeply drunk), can take all the credit these days.

But it's always been around, or at least from great antiquity; is the so-called Venus of Willendorf a fertility symbol or ancient wanking material? It doesn't do much for me, but times were different then.

Scholars of the subject have declared that the Golden Age of pornography was between 1650 and 1800, mainly in France; that was when literary pornography really began to flourish. And the interesting thing about it was that it was highly political: a call to arms against the hypocrisy of the church and the ruling classes.

Pornography has always been rebellious, subversive, anti-authority. It's in its bones, so to speak. No one, apart from a few weirdos who scour the obscurer parts of the net, is going to get their rocks off on stories of men and women in legitimate married bliss sexually pleasuring each other in a meaningful and fulfilling way. We want the squire seducing the maid, the mistress depraving the stable-hand, the Mother Superior debauching the novice nun. It has to be naughty in context as well as in deed. (Of course, the idea of a solitary woman taking her clothes off etc. is quite naughty enough for many men. And I hope you will forgive me if this discussion largely confines itself to pornography as consumed by heterosexual men. I can discourse with authority on no other kind.) The earliest work of 'modern' pornography, *The Ragionamenti of Aretino*, has its lewdest scenes in a convent; this is what makes it fun, and indeed funny. It is almost as much a work of satire as it is of one-handed literature. (As for masturbation: imagine the difference in the history and philosophy of the human race if our arms (I first wrote this sentence with the words 'men's arms', for I am one of the many men who labour under the suspicion that no woman ever masturbated until about 1972) had been, like a Tyrannosaur's, too short too reach the genitalia. I wonder what the incidence of frottage in animals is, whether they go to any ingenious lengths to bring themselves off, or whether the urgent desire to so among primates is purely and solely a matter for primates. (Cf. 'Why do dogs lick their balls? Because they can.') On the other hand, if I may coin a dreadfully distasteful phrase under the circumstances, one could examine the importance or necessity of regular self-stimulation among humans by asking double hand amputees what they do about the situation, how they live with it. Sexual longing, as Diogenes was brave enough to acknowledge, is the one urgent demand on the body that lies within the body's own power to cure; and while it may be felt to be not at all the real thing—after all, people think of sex when they masturbate, not of their own masturbation — it is far better than a substitute. It is as if, when thirsty, being shown a photograph of water would cure you of your thirst. In this regard, in its involvement with the imaginative impulse, it is as if masturbation is one of those chicken-and-egg aspects of evolution: could it perhaps be that we have cultivated our imaginative capabilities by having limbs sufficiently positioned to wank off with — that conjuring up erotic images, imagining erotic scenarios, is a result of having this physical configuration? *Masturbo, ergo cogito.*)

HOGARTH's *Before* and *After*, then, is a work of anti-pornography: it shows us what sex is really like, emotionally rather than graphically (for of course, pornography shows us what sex is 'really' like, too; but 'really', not really). It shows us the comedy of sex, the deflation of its rhetoric, as it were, whereas pornography does not show us any deflation; it tends to depart the scene after the come-shot, while the member is still rigid, and not looking like a withered balloon. Nature has not taught us how to cope with the aftermath of sex; its teleology is all about getting us there, fertilising the egg; we are driven by a demented frenzy up till then (that is, as Woody Allen just about said, if we're doing it right); after that, we can look after ourselves. Which is perhaps one reason why we're monogamous (pace the old rhyme, 'higamous hogamous, woman monogamous; hogamous higamous, men are polygamous'): post-coital awkwardness is diminished considerably if the coition has been with someone you've been doing it with forever. Then again, matrimony isn't fun: all comedies end with a marriage. (Matrimony can be funny, but only if the couple bickers; but that doesn't at all mean that it can be fun.)

But all this simply shows the pathetic nature of male desire. Women have more fun than men when it comes to sex. And when they don't have it, they don't suffer the horrible, aching pangs of longing that men do. This is what men are like when they are deprived of sex (it's from the song 'Nothing Like a Dame', the Rodgers and Hammerstein composition from *South Pacific*. Everyone on earth can hum the first few words, but few know the rest):

We feel ev'ry kind of feelin',
But the feelin' of relief
We feel hungry as the wolf felt
When he met Red Hiding-hood
What don't we feel?
We don't feel good!

Tiresias, who was not, in any sense, a figure of fun, but who knew about one crucial aspect of it better than anyone else alive, spent half his life as a woman, a condition that allowed him to answer a question that had been bugging Zeus ever since the creation: namely, whether men or women achieved more pleasure from the sexual act; women had nine times for fun than men, answered Tiresias, a response that infuriated Zeus's wife so much — it gave away the greatest, most strategically-held secret of her sex — that she blinded him. What, goes the old joke, is the most fun you can have with your clothes on? Sex — with your clothes on. And women, remember, are having nine times more fun at it than men, clothed or not. It was Elephantis, a woman, after all, who is said to have produced the world's first licentious books, i.e. pornography; her mythological prototype was Astyanassa, Helen of Troy's servant, who is said to have written a book called *On the Postures for Intercourse*. (It is not too hard a leap of the imagination to presume that Helen might have been the dedicatee of the book, and that conversations between the two furnished at least some of the details of the book; and so, along with Helen's legendary beauty, her sexual know-how would have made her absolutely irresistible. It may not have just been her face that launched a thousand ships. The Trojan War, and indeed the whole of Western literature, may have been started by sexual knowledge, being great in bed — a rare fit between Hellenic and Jewish mythology (if we assume that that was the most devastating knowledge the forbidden fruit imparted). And Achilles's anger, which sets *The Iliad* in motion, is based on Agamemnon's theft of Achilles's captured concubine, a rape of a rape.)

Elephantis was well-known as the creator of an instructive and erotic manual (the word 'manual' here seeming particularly appropriate); the Roman comic poet Martial cited her in his *Epigrams* and *Priapea*. Tiberius, the father of Caligula, was a noted rake. From Suetonius's life of Tiberius: 'On retiring to Capri he made himself a private sporting-house, where sexual extravagances were practised for his secret pleasure. Bevies of girls and young men, whom he had collected from all over the empire as adepts in unnatural practices [*et exoletorum greges monstrosique concubitus repertores*], and known as *spintriae*, would perform before him in groups of three, to excite his waning passions. A number of small rooms were furnished with the most indecent pictures and statuary obtainable, also certain erotic manuals from Elephantis in Egypt; the inmates of the establishment would know exactly what was expected of them.'

It has all been downhill from there. Since Ovid was exiled to the shithole of Tomis in 8AD by Augustus, for writing elegantly dirty poetry, advice for seducers, and probably witnessing something in the corridors of power that he shouldn't have, sex has ceased to be fun. It's been too much of a problem. Everything about it has been funny — but that is small consolation. There have been occasional attempts to break out of this state. The 1960s, for instance, were meant to have been a time of sexual freedom; after the buttoned-up disaster of the Victorian experiment, which lasted (with a short break for wartime) until 1963, it may well have seemed like that. Do I really need to quote Larkin's lines on the subject here? Surely everyone knows them. (Oh, all right then: 'Sexual intercourse began/In 1963/Between the ending of the Chatterly Ban/And the Beatles' first LP.' I quote from memory, but I think that's right.)

The seeds of the licence of the 1960s were planted earlier than we think, and the idea has remained the same throughout the ages. Dionysus was also called 'Liber', making the link with liberty etymologically explicit; and libertines were originally freethinkers, not sexual buccaneers. The idea that sexual freedom is politically urgent is not an attitude that survives in the West now (the feminist position, which it is hard to argue with, is that men will say anything if they think it will get them laid); to seek those who believe it, you have to examine the pronouncements of those who are against political and sexual liberty: 'Advocates of ... sexual licence, which undermines the family, are advocates ... of perpetual instability and disorder,' claimed Norman Tebbit in the *Spectator* (25 November 2000). If only. Wagner's second opera, rarely performed now, is *Das Liebesverbot* (1836), based loosely on *Measure for Measure*; a ban on premarital sex is imposed by the authorities. The opera as a whole is a celebration of free love, making an explicit connection with it and insurrection which would have driven Norman Tebbit to apoplexy. Or take, for example, a less surprising hedonist, Casanova, the benign hedonist, the fun-seeker, par excellence. In the words of one of his many biographers and portraitists, 'Life, for him, is an entertainment, a joyful drama: a *dramma giocoso*. He admits to being intrepid, thoughtless, avid in his pursuit of sensual or intellectual enjoyment, and ready to violate all the laws that would curb his unfettered pleasure.' (This from Stefan Zweig's marvellous book about Casanova, published by Pushkin. Get it.) He announces, at one point, that he is 'Venetian, and free in the fullest sense of the word', a remark that can be unpacked as follows: that the lucky circumstance of his birth in a powerful, wealthy and beautiful city — a nexus of characteristics and circumstances that could not be repeated anywhere else, Venetians occupying a very particular rung on the ladder of the world's societies — means that he has the example of endless amusement, of carnival, of the advertisement of sensual pleasures continually in front of him, to be taken or not as he wishes, and that even his relatively low birth (to an actress, and a specialist in optics who was once an actor) will not prevent him from rising to the highest courts in the land, or in other lands, if he should choose; and that his freedom is yet more than just the freedom of one born into a rich society, it is a freedom of attitude, a freedom in which he will indulge his own tastes and inclinations in spite of the law and custom. His full freedom is in enjoying himself, and making others enjoy themselves too, if he can.

Casanova lived his life according to the opportunities for pleasure it gave him. 'Time spent in amusement cannot be called wasted. The time to be shunned is time spent in boredom.' Although while I think that this remark is sincerely meant, it is only just to place it in context: it is part of an ongoing attempt to seduce a woman of not only extraordinary beauty but haughtiness, one who has been treating him with utter disdain. 'But I was convinced that, for her, I was nothing. It was too much. I knew that I was something, and I meant that she should know it too.' And later, after he has delivered the apophthegm cited above, and so at least on the way to being noticed: 'She did not hate me and she did not love me, that was all; and, being very young and fond of a laugh, she had chosen me to amuse herself with, as she might with a jumping jack.' This is yet another of his tokens of honesty: that he not only accepts that other women might only exist as objects for his pleasure to light upon, but that by the same token, he exists as a plaything for others. Ganders do not as a rule accept the proposition that the same sauce applies to them as to geese. That Casanova accepts this without rancour or outrage is a clear indication that what he has to say about pleasure is to be believed.

There are various kinds of lust. There was Pan, goat-boy fornicator, who taught the shepherds in Arcadia to masturbate, and so ease their loneliness and frustration; we know when he died, and therefore when Fun died, because Plutarch records the event:

> I have heard the words of a man who was not a fool nor an impostor. … He said that once upon a time, in making a voyage to Italy, he embarked on a ship carrying freight and many passengers. It was already evening when, near the Echinades Islands, the wind dropped, and the ship drifted near Paxi. Almost everybody was awake, and a good many had not finished their after-dinner wine. Suddenly from the island of Paxi was heard the voice of someone loudly calling Thamus, so that all were amazed. Thamus was an Egyptian pilot, not known by

name even to many on board. Twice he was called and made no reply, but the third time he answered; and the caller, raising his voice, said, 'When you come opposite to Palodes, announce that Great Pan is dead.' ... So, when he came opposite Palodes, and there was neither wind nor wave, Thamus, from the stern, looking toward the land, said the words as he had heard them: 'Great Pan is dead.' Even before he had finished, there was a great cry of lamentation, not of one person, but of many, mingled with exclamations of amazement.

The Greeks had a personification of the uncontrollable phallus in the form of Priapus, the son of, appropriately enough, Bacchus and Venus. Priapus was distinguished by his enormous member, and was a particular favourite of the Lampascenians, a people, according to Lemprière, 'naturally idle and indolent', and so I hope fittingly saluted here. The Lampascenians, during their festivities, 'gave themselves up to every lasciviousness and impurity'. Priapus, a rural god with much in common with Pan, was for a while sacked by the Lampascenians, 'on account of the freedom he took with their wives'. (There is here, as in so much early Greek myth, no difference between history and what we now know as myth.) But the people of Lampascus were shortly afterwards afflicted with a disease of the genitals, and welcomed him back, building temples to him and organising festivities with an even greater will than before.

Gods were worshipped not, as now, necessarily because they were seen to be wise; they were worshipped in order to be appeased. Priapus may have been adopted and bowdlerized by the Romans as a god of gardens and — that pervasive euphemism — 'fertility', but his character was well known enough. (A statue of Priapus was a common feature in Roman gardens: the idea was to deter burglars. Enter the grounds without permission, was the implication, and the god will sodomise you.) The *satyr* play — from which, eventually, the term 'satire' evolves — was characterized by the joyous display of outlandishly huge, erect penises by the half-human divinities, who when first encountered in Greek literature (Hesiod's *Theogony*) they are characterised as being 'useless at work'. But this is no simple comic romp, a fustian Benny Hill; it is an invocation of the darkest Dionysiac rites, of orgiastic frenzy and destruction. It survives, in modern iconography, in the enormous pudenda of Aubrey Beardsley's illustrations, the crude, urgent graffiti on a toilet wall, or the masks with phallic noses worn by Alex and his Droogs in Kubrick's film of *A Clockwork Orange*, prior to the rape of one of their victims; or in the sculpture of an enormous cock and balls with which Alex murders another (changed from a statue of a naked girl in the original novel). Priapism may have been funny, but it certainly had its sinister and vicious aspect to it, and early drama and myth accommodated the character of the rapist. The prime example was, of course, Zeus; but it took some while before humans were portrayed with the same insatiable lusts. The theatre was looked at as enough of a pit of licentiousness by the church as it was. Tirso de Molina is accepted as the creator of the Don Juan story (a rumour has it that he somewhat appropriately sold his soul to the devil in exchange for fame); he starts off as a heartless seducer; by the time he appears in this country, in Shadwell's *The Libertine*, he is unambiguously wicked, gripped by purely malicious, almost abstract desire: 'Let me see, here lives a Lady: I have seen Don Octavio haunting about this house, and making private signs to her. I never saw her face, but am resolv'd to enjoy her, because he likes her; besides, she's another woman.' (It was Shadwell's Don John — as he was called — who first used the phrase 'in lust with', which achieved a popularity among American teenagers in the mid-1990s. It is also interesting that the play appears at around the same time the word 'fun' is entering the language, although I have not noticed it in the play.)

Don Juan's name may have survived for centuries as a shorthand for uncaring sexual rapaciousness, but in the twentieth century, Michel Foucault was, perhaps for personal reasons, suspicious of Don Juan's priapism: 'Underneath the great violator of the rules of marriage — stealer of wives, seducer of virgins, the shame of families, and an insult to husbands and fathers — another personage can be glimpsed: the individual driven, in spite of himself, by the sombre madness of sex. Underneath the libertine, the pervert...There were two great systems conceived by the West for governing sex: the law of marriage and the order of desires — and the life of Don Juan overturned them both. We shall leave it to psychoanalysts to speculate whether he was homosexual, narcissistic, or impotent.' (*The History of Sexuality, Vol. I.*)

Foucault's suspicion that Don Juan was not as heterosexual as he himself asserts (and as all the literary evidence explicitly attests) is revealing, and not just about Foucault, who was a homosexual of legendary appetites. It's another indication that there has always been something effeminate about pleasure, about licence, about Folly, even in its most heterosexual incarnations. It is crucial to remember that until the mid-eighteenth century, women were considered to be as sexually rapacious as men, if not more so. Much has been made, too, of the ancient world's casual attitude to male homosexuality, although if there is a conclusion to be drawn about that it may as well refer to an appreciation of beardlessness — a smooth motion of skin against skin — as a delight in the specifically male form. Lucian imagines Hera's fury with Zeus for having seduced Ganymede (and it's interesting, too, that Ganymede is seen as a plaything, someone who exists only to have fun with):

H: ... And the other day, you, the king and father of all, laid aside your aegis and thunderbolt, and sat down playing dice with him, you with that great beard on your face! I see it all. Don't think you're hoodwinking me ... that Phrygian softie. Oh, the effeminate creature!

Just as our ideas of fun invariably involve doing something that we do not normally do, this could be said to be our sexuality's idea of fun: a holiday from the normal proclivities. This is the comedic aspect of the penis's demands, its any-port-in-a-storm potential, nowadays in the West not so prevalent, now that our sexual orientation is such a matter of serious, almost political consequence. The notion that male priapism can readily extend itself to homosexuality might disturb many men today, but it would not have surprised Ovid, who in his Fasti tells us 'an ancient, playful tale' which tells us why celebrants of the rites of Faunus — Pan — do so naked. Pan had decided to try and force himself on a particular mortal woman, but, unknown to him, she had, for her amusement, dressed her lover up in her own clothes. In the dead of night ('it was midnight. What does vicious lust not attempt?'), with everyone drunkenly asleep, he finds a form dressed in her soft clothes. 'His swollen groin was harder than horn. / He begins lifting the dress from its hem below.' He is fought off, lights are lit, he's seen 'whimpering on the hard ground', and everyone finds it all immensely funny. 'Since clothes fooled him, the god hates deceptive clothing / And summons people naked to his rites.' But the essence of the story is the comedy of sexual confusion, as it is with Lucian, some years later, who imagines this dialogue between Dionysus and Apollo:

But now as for Priapus — I'll tell you something really funny. The other day — it was in Lampascus — I was passing the city, when he invited me home with him, and put me up for the night. Now we'd gone to sleep in his dining-room, after and were pretty well soaked, when about midnight up gets our bold lad — but I'm ashamed to tell you.

A: And made an attempt on you, Dionysus?
D: Something like that.
A: How did you deal with the situation?
D: What could I do but laugh?

The scene is echoed much later in Casanova's memoirs, when a randy Sultan — with whom Casanova has been watching, unseen, a group of women bathing — tries to seduce the famed (hetero-)sexual adventurer; as it turns out, the Sultan gets his way with the aroused Casanova:

'Ismail, faint with delight, not only convinced me that I should not restrain my-self, but encouraged me to surrender to the effects which the voluptuous sight could not but produce in my soul, by himself setting the example. Like him, I found myself reduced to making the best of the object beside me to extinguish the flame kindled by the three sirens'—although these Sirens were silent, and unconscious of the men they were so inflaming; but the link between the Sirens and passionate desire, as noted by Bacon, is reinforced—'and Ismail triumphed when he found that his proximity condemned him to take the place of the distant object to which I could not attain. I also had to submit to his taking turnabout. It would have been impolite in me to refuse; then, too, I should have shown myself ungrateful, a thing which is not in my nature. ...The departure of the three sirens ended the orgy; as for us, since we did not know what to say to each other, we simply laughed.' The reaction is the same as Dionysus's: what can you do but laugh? It is as if they have hit upon one of the essences of comedy.

No law, though, says there can't be another Casanova. Or even that Casanova has to be male. We need one, now. Any volunteers?

This is a disorganised extract from Nicholas Lezard's book on Fun,
to be completed soon (really)

GEE VAUCHER

ICONS

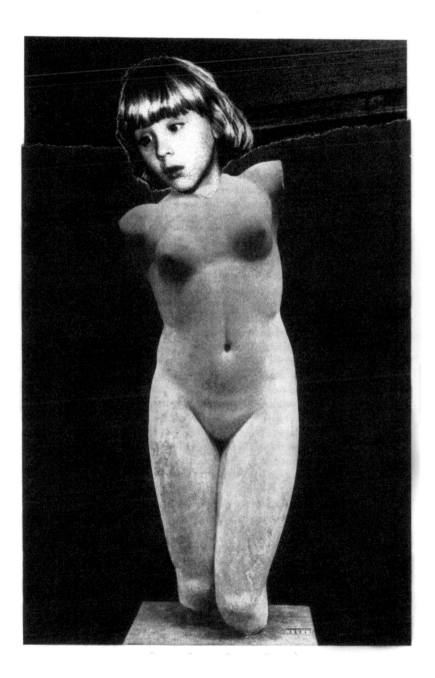

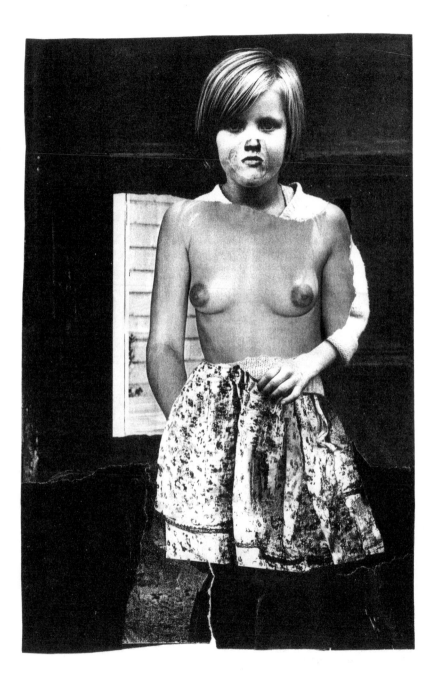

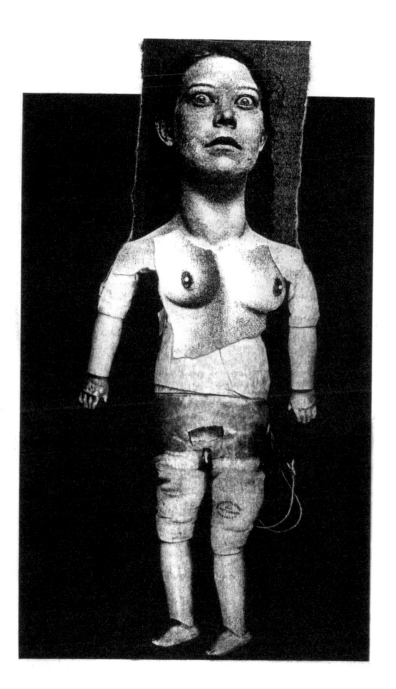

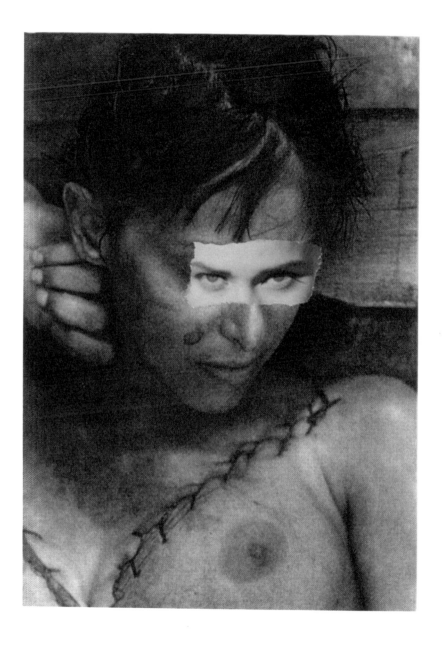

I'm Waiting for my Manhood: Neil Boorman in Soho.
Picture by Daniel Pemberton

SEX LIES

Neil Boorman isn't getting it

EX. TONNES OF IT ABOUT, ONLY I DON'T SEEM TO BE GETTING
much of it myself. Not the sort that everyone else seems to be getting, in any
case. Don't get me wrong, my love life is not a disaster; I have long
settled into a satisfying schedule of indoor fireworks. I would be satisfied, only I'm
constantly reminded that other peoples' sex lives go with a bigger bang — all giant
Catherine wheels and Jean-Michel Jarre lasers.

In the newspapers, celebrities kiss and tell about their wild dalliances with other
glamorous alpha-beings. In the magazines, journalists embark on intrepid missions
to the underbelly of British sex (men's mags), and run how-to manuals on the
continual spicing up of one's love life (women's). During the dramas on television,
one leading character is guaranteed to rip the panties off a co-star in the
toilets of a fancy restaurant. Ever since 9½ *Weeks*, any film of 15 certificate or more
must include a sex scene that involves food fetishism, light bondage and
multiple orgasms. And we all know what devilry befouls the highways of the
internet. Everywhere I turn, people seem to be pushing boundaries, bending
genders and swapping roles. Everyone except me.

The situation might be easier if I actually knew someone how enjoyed one of
these modern sex lives; they could supply me with the occasional titbit of salacious
gossip, and I could gain some vicarious pleasure from it all. Barring one friend,
who likes to frustrate me with her same-sex fantasies (exactly none of which she
has followed through), my mates' pub chat is rather low on illicit hotel threesomes
or ritualistic orgies. No whipping, no dogging, no rinding*. Which leads me to the
question, is anybody having the glamorous, adventurous, voluminous sex that we
hear so much about?

Despite the continuous groans of ecstasy escaping from the media, I rather
suspect that the answer is no. Like so many of the visions of life that glare at us
from TV screens and billboards, modern sex is entirely the work of fiction, stylised
dreams concocted by think tanks in advertising agencies and Hollywood studios.

---

* I'm not even sure what rinding is. I think that it involves bacon rind and string, but I cannot be sure.

Sex has long been a stick with which industry has beaten the consumers' brow to manufacture desire, but the modern publicity machine has become so pervasive that its vision of life defines what it is to be normal. And so the stylised vision of sex, all satin blindfolds and ice cubes on the nipples, becomes the apparent norm. Everyone, it would appear, is doing it, so why aren't we?

To be sexually active is to be normal. To explore one's fantasies (within the boundaries of good taste) is healthy. To admit to anything less is an admission of failure and a sign of inadequacy. As a man, I must maintain a voracious sexual appetite and perform mutually satisfying routines with the precision of a porn star. My partner must be willing to transform herself into a burlesque madam, carefully negotiating the boundaries between adventurous lover and all-out slut, all the while packaged in expensive designer underwear. All of which makes the traditional half-hour missionary fumble, followed by a kiss and a cuddle, rather mundane. The bar has been raised and we must stretch ourselves accordingly; to aspire to anything less is to let down both yourself and your partner.

As a child of the early Eighties, I was brought up on far lower sexual aspirations. With no internet and a tightly restricted media, my sexual entertainment was confined to grubby copies of Paul Raymond's *Escort* and *Razzle* found in the woods of my local park (to this day, I cannot understand why second hand pornography is always to be found in the woods). In these magazines, the chubby girls of Leicester flaunted their boobs in the car park of Sainsbury while readers' wives flashed their hairy bits, bent over formica tables in naff MFI kitchens with evening's stew bubbling on the hob. This being the pre-Photoshop era, the girls had pasty white flesh, rippled with light cellulite, marked by un-groomed pubic hair. The outfits were straight out of Primark (when Primark was seconds only to Quality Seconds in the lowest divisions of cool). Girls struck poses of the *Carry On* variety; naughty but nice glimpses of the forbidden. The readers' letters, though obviously the work of fiction, were based in the real world — naughty housewives seducing the window cleaner, grubby mechanics taking payment for MOTs on the back seat of the Capri. The modern sexual fantasy is set atop luxury speedboats, with flawless models sipping Crtistal champagne in Gucci bikinis, as brought to us by the endless bling of MTV.

Sexual decadence occupies so much of the subtext of advertising that it becomes a form of oppression, a source of anxiety. I see an advert for Walls Sensation ice creams. In the adverts, a woman slowly fellates the tip of the ice cream as Barry White purrs to the backing track. It reminds me that eating Sensations is sensual experience, and that I should eat one when I next feel like indulging myself. But it also reminds me that there are apparently millions of beautiful, glamorous people engaging in sexual acts right now, the intensity and fabulousness of which I could only dream of. The initial sensation is pleasant, but the titillation soon subsides by a wave of disappointment, as the reality of my own, rather banal, life becomes clear. The solution to this misery, it would seem, is to buy more ice cream.

Having only recently escaped from centuries of sexual repression, us English people have become rather nouveau riche in regards to sex — flaunting ourselves at one another, wearing our sexuality on our sleeves, gossiping endlessly about who's doing what to whom — onspicuous attempts to keep up with the chandelier-swinging Joneses. As ever, the Joneses are themselves the stuff of myth; merely mirrors to our own anxious aspirations. The modern myths of sexual glamour tend to enjoy greater shelf lives than most media-driven fallacies because, sex being a largely private act, one can boast, infer and assume without having to prove a thing. If one claims to have bought a new Ferrari, friends will naturally expect to see some evidence. Common decency prohibits the requesting of proof of a three in a bed romp. And so, the media-driven charade abounds, reinforcing the myth that the cornerstones of normal modern sex are frequency, variety and debauchery. Which in real life is as accurate as the readers' letters in Razzle.

Allow me to break from tradition then, and admit to the world that my sex life falls way short of the modern expectations. Moreover, that I don't really care. I am prepared to commit social suicide and admit to a number of embarrassing personal truths. The more I admit to them, the less embarrassing they become.

1. I sometimes go for weeks without sex, and it doesn't bother me.

2. I didn't loose my virginity until I was 19; it was rather disappointing when I did.

3. Far from being a turn on, both ice cubes and candle wax on the extremities doesn't feel very nice at all.

4. During my bachelorhood, I felt lonelier during one-night stands than staying at home on my own.

5. I've eaten dozens of Walls Sensations ice creams, and not once has the experience reminded me of sex.

Neil Boorman's book Bonfire of the Brands *is out now on Canongate*

PAGE 3 in the COUNTRY

Three go wild in the country
with Tom Beard

Shot at Richmond Park and on the Thames at Richmond

❖

Models:
Anna Tavanner
Krystal Gohel
Alex Sin-Wise
from
IMM

❖

Stylist:
Gemma Cairney

❖

With thanks to Coco de Mer *and* Beyond Retro

❖

Coco de Mer
23 Monmouth Street, London, WC2H 9DD
Tel: 020 7836 8882

Beyond Retro
58–59 Great Marlborough Street, London, W1 F7JY
Tel: 0207 434 1406

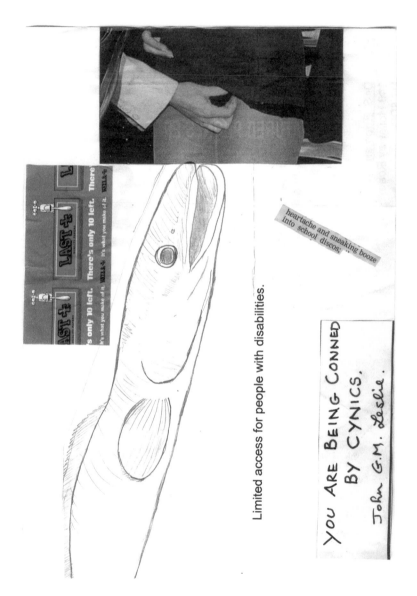

heartache and sneaking booze into school discos;

Limited access for people with disabilities.

YOU ARE BEING CONNED BY CYNICS.

John G.M. Leslie.

From the pen of
Jock Scot

JOCK'S TOP SEX TIPS

CHEESE

I've always liked cheese. I can talk to you as long as you like … [about cheese].
Sex and food are very closely related. Cheese is sex for grown-up pop stars.
Alex James, ex-Blur bassman, farmer and cheesemaker

IF, AS PLATO THOUGHT, 'LOVE IS THE PURSUIT OF THE WHOLE',
then those of us unfettered by the straitjacket of Political Correctness would
ribaldly counter that 'sex is the pursuit of the hole.' Or, in the case of *Le Grand
Fromage*, Alex James, 'the holes in the cheese.' Of course I presume that Alex is
comparing the taste of cheese to sex . Its great variety of flavours, from the subtle
blandness of Laughing Cow to the heavyweight tastebud rocker of Gorgonzola, and
not the smell, which can be redolent of stained underwear, unwashed socks and
worse. But it is often courting disappointment to be presumptious, especially in the
case of SEX.

Many's the night when I have sat in a public house, sipping happily at a pint of
Guinness and chanting the mantra: 'I'm on a promise. I'm on a promise,' only to
discover some hours, pints and pounds later, that my current squeeze has either
changed her mind, despite my protestations that it's her mind I love her for, or that
she's got the painters in. Sex rule number one: Never presume. But I digress.

I suppose I was fortunate to have been born in 1952, 'cos come the late 1960s,
when my hormones were ricocheting around my expanding mind and the horn
was rising, morals, attitudes and opportunities were increasingly in favour of the
young man trying to get his end away. The girls could easily obtain the contracep-
tive pill and the only STD's you had to watch out for were things like the clap,
VD, gonorrhea, herpes, NSU, crabs, genital warts etc. Killer diseases like HIV-
Aids had yet to be introduced to society by the CIA as a means of controlling gays
and black people.

I managed to break my duck on a wet and muddy cricket pitch with a 'popular' local lass called Linda Goodthighs, one Sunday night after the Bible Class Disco.

I was surprised and disappointed with the physical reality of the act. After the years of hearsay, ignorance and hype etc., no wonder it was a let-down.

But remember, practice makes perfect.

❖

FUN

TRY and keep it 'fun'. In my experience, if you can make them laugh, that's a good start, you're half way there. You can laugh girls into bed and if it's a disaster, laugh it off. The sex act is such an odd thing you've got to laugh! Sex is, after all, overrated. As John Lydon said, 'Sex is three and a half minutes of squelching noises.'

❖

MEDIA

SEX sells. My former boss, the late Auberon Waugh, in his days as editor of *The Literary Review*, insisted on having the word **SEX** in bold type on the cover of every issue. He rightly believed that the promise of sex sold more copies. Whether or not there were any sex-related articles within the pages of the magazine mattered not a jot.

Nowadays the media, in its various forms, is always working the sex angle, selling the poor mug-punter news of the latest sex-based carry ons of the media whores they presume live lifestyles that the average drone-commuter aspires to. This is where you want to tread carefully. They are printing cynical, sensational half-truths, backed up by a legion of showbiz lawyers, selling you dreams which the more gullible then compute as a lifestyle (which bears no relation to their daily lives) that they are missing out on. So just transcend the bullshit and get on with enjoying whatever comes your way. Drink, drugs etc.

❖

BOOZE

I SUPPOSE the main barrier to my own enjoyment of a happy sex life was my weakness for a jar or two. Throughout my life I have enjoyed getting drunk at every available opportunity, especially if free booze was available. There is nothing more sobering than to have a young lass you have always thought attractive in the extreme sidle up to you one evening, years after having first been introduced, and have her whisper in your shell-like, 'I've always fancied you.' This will usually happen just before her multi-millionaire husband appears at her elbow to remove her from your incredulous presence to escort the still-smitten vision to his waiting, top-of-the-range Mercedes for the drive back to their luxury town house in Chelsea.

What I'm saying is that opportunities for dalliance will present themselves, so try to be sober enough to decipher the signals. And that goes whether or not you move in the rarefied social circles I occasionally did in my days as a drunken young man about town.

❖

CURVES

BACK in the day when I had a full wallet and a full head of hair SEX symbols were curvaceous, untouchable screen goddesses (fill in your own favourites here). Nowadays, what have we? Mrs. Beckham and Katie 'Jordan' Price. A barmy ex-pop singer who couldn't sing and a grotesque, inflatable media-whore, as 'role models' for legions of hard-drinking, non-thinking slappers. Well lads, you get what you pay for. Personally, I'd rather spend the evening trying to have a conversation with Goldenballs about the night Real Madrid won La Liga.

But do not despair! There's someone for everyone, even if she looks like Julie Burchill or Vanessa Feltz. There are no end of desperate, confused young lads queueing up to try and put their arms around them. Some men actually prefer the larger woman, and the older ones too. Apparently in Milan there is a bordello where the working girls are all aged over sixty-five. Whatever turns you on.

Mathilde Lasseny by Lindsay Brunnock

STORIES

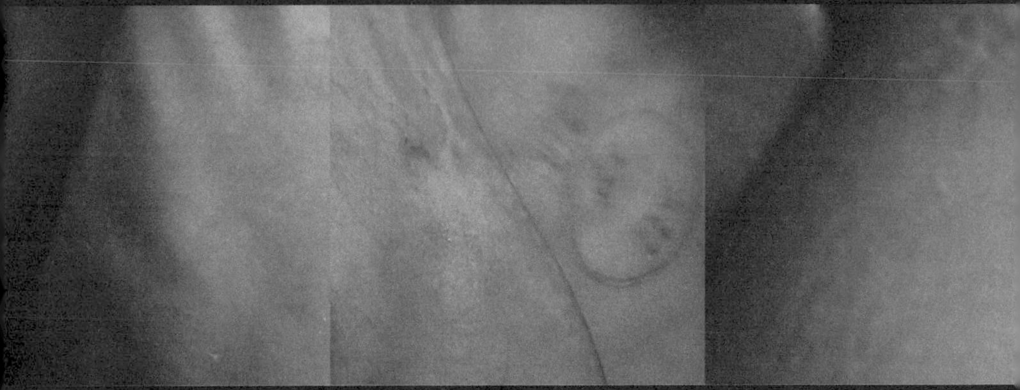

] BRACKETPRESS [

www.bracketpress.co.uk

deride those who seek
Tell them it's all a dream
Just chat,

Let's fuck.

Let's chat

THE NATURE OF REJECTION
– fucking smart-arse –

A Treatise by Penny Rimbaud

HELENE'S CUNT

†

That one smile, like a feather traced across the temple, a cobweb turned into the wind, like waking-blood trickling through the cerebral cortex.

THE MIGRAINE, JESUS, THE MIGRAINE.

You tricked me again. You tricked me with your kind-heartedness: again and again and again. Will I ever learn? I hadn't wanted to go away. It was you who said that I should.

FUCKHEAD

"We need to have a little chat."

You claimed it was only a suggestion, but I didn't like the inflection you placed on 'little'. It seemed too considered, so I took it as a rejection. Why else would the need exist?

"Now."

And that was emphatic, unpleasantly so. But, surely, everything was subject to redefinition? It was always worth a second thought, a second look, a second opinion.

"Do you hear me?"

"Yes, I hear you talking."

"We need to talk."

"Go ahead."

"Christ, I don't know why I bother."

Which was also stated emphatically.

No wonder I drifted.

"OVER HERE"

It was at breakfast time that you would adopt the role of philosopher in the safe knowledge that my only interest at that time of day was coffee and cigarettes. It was a cheap trick.

"WE ARE FINITE. WE ARE THE VERB."
"UH?"

"NOW THEN, LET'S TALK ABOUT IT."

More often than not your hair carried the scent of overlit beauty salons or underlit massage parlours: fleshy-warm and wild in a flashy-worn and mild sort of a way.

"IT'S IN THE DOING."

The music is blaring: local radio, mid-Atlantic drawl, pussy-love and innuendo.

YES, SIR, WHO'S MY BABY?
(mmm, maybe)

I had wanted to write about Descartes,
but I couldn't find my fucking spectacles.

P U S S Y

"Yeah, I'll call you brother if you'll just be my all-night lover."

"Okay, Babe."

WOW, BIG MOUTH,
FOUND YOU AT LAST!

"NOW THEN, WHAT DID YOU SAY?"

"OOH, OOH, SHAG ME, BABY."

You roll across the carpet onto the pillows, your back arched over the soft down. You slip a finger into your mouth, chew at your own sweet flesh as your eyes dart in and out of dawn and dusk. You have a dream, inject it into my blood-stream. It rushes through me in a turmoil, finds my cock, bloats it something nasty.

THIS IS THE THORNY VICE ROD

Time flies by you as I reach for your cunt. I feel the moistness. You look me in the face, your eyes now unfocused. I am lost in the garden. The petals fall all around. Your mouth breaks into a smile. I gently work my fingers across your wet crack, reach with my other hand for your button-like nipples. They are hard and precious like pearls. I snatch the bodice from the floor, roll it into a bandage. Your jaw tenses as if you know already of the gag.

"You can't," you whisper, your voice deep and sonorous as if your throat was coated with chocolate, "yes, you can."

My fingers slip into your cunt, and I feel the muscles break into mild spasm. I lower my face to yours, nibble your quivering lips.

"I won't," I sigh, "yes, I will."

YOU MOUTHLESS WANDERER

"Oh yes, yes. No. Oh yes."

LIKE THE BATTLEFIELDS OF TIME

You are the extension, the pumping veins of my aching cock. You are the martyr, ready for the stake, the orchestration of dreams.

"But don't dreams express the paucity of our imagination?" I'd asked, ready still to make the changes.

You had laughed as if I wasn't serious.

"Aren't they?" I'd repeated, irritated by your lack of response.

"WHO THE FUCK DO YOU THINK YOU ARE,
FUCKING DESCARTES?"

Who the fuck is Descartes anyway? And where are my spectacles? Now then, let's see.

"Hi, call me Tina, and I'm yours."

Jesus, those tits, now they're WORTH a second thought.

Let me just unclasp that strap, unclasp that …

WOW
HUMDINGERS

What a march, no, match. What a match. Hey, let's chat.

"Tina? Tina? Tell me, how d'you manage to draw breath with that meatmarket hanging off your chest? It's an abattoir of sheer cunning. You make me hard, baby, real hard."

"Ooh, then let me taste it and suck it before you spunk in my tight white pussy."

"No, babe, I want it my way."

"Okay, fuck me from behind then I'll clean your cock."

"No."

"I'll sit astride your face and let it flow."

"No."

"I'm a virgin pussy begging for my first fuck. I'm looking for a good hard cock. Oh, I need it badly."

Wow, now you're talking.

I LIKE ALL THIS CHIT CHAT.
I COULD DIG IT.

Step aside, you men of steel, I am the predator. Let me in with the poleaxe. I am the exterminator. Let me in with the poleaxe. Yes, yes, yes. Let me in with the
P   O   L   E   A   X   E

Careful now, careful, ease it, baby. Squeeze it, baby. Please it, baby. Mmm, yes, yes, that's dandy. Let the good times roll, my sugar candy, let them roll right randy into that little box of yours, so handy.

OKAY,
WHO'S MY BABY NOW?
VIR-GIN
(you meat market)

UGH

Chat? Fucking chat? I was drowning in that great big ocean of pleasures, my syrup. You were the principle, my sweet, the ethic. I came to you with my sorrows and my spunk, full like barberry juice. You were torn. You were the particular, the specimen, the witch's cat. You were worn. Ooosh, whoosh.

I'm going to return: re-turn. Well, well …

GOTTA TALK

"Passion?" you asked, "What of passion?"
"The divine conflict of opposites."

And I'd bend again and draw your breast into my mouth until I too gagged. You would squirm a little squirm. I'd push open your legs and your cunt would be red and raw like the butcher's last strike. I'd suck on this cut and look out across the savanna. The wildebeests had been destroyed, gunned down. The vultures had retreated to the glaciers. Kilimanjaro was wrapped in snow. Hemingway snored a snore, and the ship broke loose.

Now I am alone, the savage painted in gore. I am the art.

BIGC□CK & BALLS TO PICASS□

DREAMS ARE SO-O-O-O-O-O
GOD-DAMNED CHEAP

YES

"We need to talk."
"Okay, talk then. Talk, talk, talk, but have you seen my spectacles?"

D E S C A R T E S

"They're on your head."

Descartes sat at his desk, looked out of the window, looked out across autumnal skies. Descartes had got his thinking-cap on. He looked stylish in a philosophical kind of way. Descartes thought he had a thought, then, with infinite care, he lifted his quill from the ink-bottle and wrote down what he thought was the thought he'd thought:

"My God, I am."

Then he replaced his quill in the ink-bottle, relishing the vinegary scent that drifted up from the disturbed fluid.

"Words, fine words, but somehow not quite right," he mumbled to himself, a faintly ironic smile breaking across his lined face (but someone had to squash the ants).

Descartes sat at his desk, looked out of the window, looked out across rosy autumnal skies. Descartes thought a thought, then, with infinite care, he lifted his quill from the ink-bottle and wrote down his thought:

"But if I am, who the hell is God?
Maybe I should try wearing a fez."

It was a form of revisionism.

Descartes rubbed his hands together, had another thought, which might have been a feeling, and wondered for a while whether he should keep it to himself or smuggle it down to the village. Rejecting both options, he then very slowly brought his hand across the desk, narrowly missing the long, white feather of the quill, and gently but purposefully rang the bell. Very shortly afterwards the door opened, and Hélène tip-tœd into the room. She did not like to disturb her master.

"Come here," Descartes said authoritively, "I want to try a little experiment."

Hélène approached apprehensively. It was not often that she was subjected to a dialogue with the master, but when she was it would normally follow the same course.

"Bend over my desk," Descartes ordered, "but mind the quill, will you?" Hélène obeyed.

With an air of deep contemplation, Descartes lifted Hélène's skirt and then, equally contemplatively, pulled down her bloomers. Descartes was a contemplative kind of a man.

"Mmm," he thought, "interesting, very interesting."

Hélène could smell the vinegary scent of the ink. Something about it reminded her of her childhood, something about the huge chestnut tree that had stood in the centre of the village square. In summer, old men would congregate in the shade of the tree and talk of battles (which they had never fought), or the value of grain (of which they had little) against the value of livestock (of which they had less). There was no comparison to be made. Hélène thought of her father and the acrid smell of his underarms. His underarms had been spectacularly hairy, as if the process of evolution had somehow slowed down when it came to him. As a young child she had been fascinated by the way in which that massive bush of hair pushed out through the arm-holes of his leather jerkin. It was as if his hair was the fur of the animal from which the jerkin had been made.

Darwin had a dream that took him back to pre-consciousness. He never woke up.

"So, what is it you want to chat about?"
"Us, but I don't know where to begin."
"Begin with you."
"I don't know what to say. You never understand me."

Descartes thought for a while, looked out of the window across flesh-soft, rosy autumnal skies, and then studied Hélène's arse; they were much the same colour. It was a nice arse and no doubt about it.

Hélène could feel Descartes' eyes on her arse; they were blue and icy cold like a winter's sky. In winter the old men would only rarely sit beneath the chestnut tree, and then only for a short while. They would talk of other winters and how difficult it had been to survive them. Hélène had noticed how over the years the forest that extended beyond the village had become increasingly sparse. To gather wood, the young men had to venture further and further, which put them in danger of attack from wild animals or, even worse, from bandits. Hélène had always been afraid of the forest; it was too dark, too deep, and the bandits were known to be fierce men who *weren't* afraid of using their weapons.

MIGHTY WEIGHTY

Descartes forced his fingers into Hélène's cunt, a considered action, but one which, considering the circumstances could have been made with a little more consideration.

"I can at least try."
"No regrets?"
"Jesus, you haven't even defined the boundaries."
"There's got to be regrets."
"What about respect?"
"That too, but it's too late. You'll never change."
"Change? My life's not a commodity. I can't change my life because I am my life."
"Then change your fucking mind."

"SHARP!"
(it must have been breakfast time)

Although Hélène could feel Descartes' fingers searching around inside her cunt, she wasn't really sure whether or not she felt anything at all. When the boys from the village had fingered her she'd felt excited and become wet, but now she felt dry as the pond-bed in a summer's drought. She looked out of the window across storm-gathering skies and thought of the hay-barns and the cornfields and saw the wood-smoke drifting and heard the cattle mooing and the chickens clucking. It made her feel secure, but still she wasn't wet.

THE TERRIFYING SWISH
OF THE WHIP.
THE AWFUL THUD
OF THE CLUB.

"Hélène?"

That last time I saw you. That last sense of joy, as if the magician's dust was rubbed into my hands, and the crystals were wrapped around my brow. This was no crown of thorns. A steel pot boiled deep inside my stomach, it enlivened my inner body and fired the outer flesh. And how I smiled and ran and leapt in that joy, casting off the sallow shadows and for one moment remembering my name.

Jamie Templeton (address unknown)

A FUCKING WAGNER NO LESS

DESCARTES' FISH FINGERS

✝

Descartes slipped his fingers out of Hélène's cunt, they stunk of fish, no two ways about it: haddock or mackerel or maybe…

"Mmm, cod," he thought, nodding his head.

But still Descartes wasn't sure.

"There are some things that a man can never know," he muttered to himself.

For a while he considered jotting down this his most contemporary thought, but Hélène was leant over the note-pad, and in any case he wasn't really certain that the thought carried sufficient gravitas.

Descartes thought again, firstly looking deep into his own thoughts, and then, more agreeably, to Hélène's arse.

"I've got something here," he muttered, sniffing his fingers, and then, more excitedly, "surely an orifice is also a meeting point, both form and content. Yes, of course," at which point, with no consideration whatsoever for Hélène's feelings, he rammed his two fingers straight back into her cunt. Descartes was becoming less careful if only because after all these years he felt that he was at last onto something. The philosopher's stone was turning to gold, and his consciousness was lit up with a form of intellectual greed (but that's still no cause to be uncaring).

"Yes, yes," he mused, twisting and turning his fingers, "yes," withdrawing them, lifting them to his nose, bathing in the odour, "mmm, the index finger smells of fish, no doubt about it, but the forefinger? Very different. Now, what is it? Rabbit? Jugged hare? The spray of a tom-cat? Mmm, interesting, very interesting. Why *do* they smell so different?"

And then, just behind his head he heard the shrill whine of a mosquito. It irritated him, disturbed his thoughts. He flapped his spare hand around in the air, hoping that he might whoosh away this unwanted intruder, but it had no effect whatsoever. The mosquito continued to buzz threateningly.

"Bugger off," Descartes muttered, alarming Hélène from her reverie.

"Should I leave, sir?" she asked passively.

"No, Hélène," replied Descartes, uninterestedly patting her arse as one might the head of a lap-dog, "I'll need you to stay for a while yet."

Having finally landed on Descartes' neck, the mosquito bit, causing its victim a moment's anguish.

"Bastard," slapping his neck and then studying his hand for the squashed corpse.

The little black form was caught between his index and forefinger, framed with a tiny splash of blood. Descartes thought of the rose and the thorn, but could make nothing of it.

(In her own village, Hélène had been a giant, but Descartes knew nothing of this.)

THE WISDOM OF NIETZSCHE

✝

Your mouth, like a cock-suck, it made me forgetful. I don't like this empty bed, this lonesome head. There's nothing to turn to. Why did I have to leave you?

mmm

Jesus, it's coming back. Shiny red satin, wet at the crotch, wet and salty and hot. It's a hot twat, that's what she'd got, a hot twat. So who's a lucky girl? Who? Who? Now, let's see.

"Call me Sandie and I'm yours."
"Don't mind if I do. Who?"
"Sandie. Sandie."

And Sandie rips off her shiny red satin panties, nonchalantly tossing them into the expectant air where they are caught by the bristling breeze, carried out through the wide-open window and on across the luxuriant landscape: a diaphanous red scream looking for a mouth.

Jesus, this one's a saint.

And Sandie blinks, and spunk spurts from her every pore. She rolls onto her back, cocks a leg, brandishes the bulge of her box and pisses all over my face.

"Come on then, sucker."

WOHA NOW, SANDIE.

She's worn out and swollen from the fist, the first fist and the last fist and all those fists in between. Last supper? Nothing.

WOHA NOW.

Socrates picks his nose, Sartre sheds a tear and the giants of time know no shame (and why, indeed, should they?).

DARWIN DIES IN OBSCURITY.

So why then did you tell me to leave? Was my story not enough? You would sit in the garden and read your books, all thought and philosophy:

OKAY, SO I WANTED THE FILTH.

"This is Nietzsche," you would say. "In the mountains the shortest route is from peak to peak, but for that you must have long legs. Aphorisms should be peaks, and those to whom they are spoken should be big and tall of stature."

"Forget the words," I'd sigh, "I want action. Is that too much to ask?"

"But what will that change?" you would shrug.

"The inner landscape?"

"With your fancy for romance and criminal violence?"

"A deeper vision. A pinpointing of the soul."

"Dreams of sodomy and assassination? You're just words."

"The fire of existence."

"The extinguishing of all else."

You would pick an apple from the tree, polish it on your blouse so that the perfumes blended and rolled across the table. You would hold the apple between finger and thumb and inspect it for flaws. If it wasn't perfect, you would look around quizzi-cally as if trying to find something or someone upon which to apportion the blame, then you would toss it over the wall.

"Huh," you would mutter, "no place here for the serpent," scratching your fanny and giving me a wink, "in any case, you've always been a conference-pear-man."

"Fucking philosophers," I'd respond, feeling my cock rise.

EDEN
(but some stupid sod left the gate open)

"Hey, there's nothing to turn to. Why'd I have to go?"
"And close the door after you."

(or bomb the fuck out of it)

Look now, Jade is a straightforward cutie, a 'one look and you're stiff as a rod' cutie. She's a 'got the tits and you want them' cutie. She's a 'got the lips and you want them' cutie. Can't consider the cunt, it's too much to consider, too much to take on in one go. Jade is the sort of cutie whose name is enough. Jade, Jade, Jade and you're already half-way shooting a load into your underpants. Don't move, Jade, don't let the pout fade, Jade, don't let it fade, Jade, you cutie, you beauty.

"Jade, Jade, Jade, oooh, wow, here I go again."

RIGHT BETWEEN THE EYES

"Ooooh, don't move now, Jade, don't move."
"Yeah, call me Donna, and I'm yours."

"HUH?"

"There's no real alternative," you would admonish, finding the perfect apple, biting into it, juices running down your chin, "is there?"

"No? I don't know."

And weren't your questions clever, weren't they just so calculated? Hadn't we braved those heights together?

"Now," I'd shout, my voice echoing across the empty valley.

"I can't," you'd shout back, "I can't fucking move."

But the move was always there if only you would wait to find it.

I never really believed you would want it to end.

OKAY, SO IT WAS HELENE WHO FORGOT TO SHUT THE GATE.

SO?

4

THE MEANING OF THE BLUES

†

Oh let's chat, let's fuck. let's just chat, let's just fuck. Blah de blah de blah. Avoid questions. Deny doubt. Accept the obvious. Throw disdain at those who quest a better knowledge. Ooh yes, do it, do it, do it. Mock and deride those who seek change. Tell them it'll never happen. Tell them it's all a dream.

Just chat,   just fuck.
    Make it nice.
    Make it polite.
    Whip it and whack it,
     kick it and crack it,
   but keep it within
      the
        confines.
Let's chat.   Let's fuck.
    Flip it and flap it,
    ride it and slide it,
    suck it and muck it,
    duck it and fuck it
and when we're worn to a corpse,
let's   go for more,
          go for more,
more suck   and muck
and duck   and fuck.
It's nice, but it's got a price.
Just chat.   Just fuck.
Scream it   and cream it,
Bang   pump it,
  bang   lump it
    bang,   and dump it.
      whang
       whang
        whang.

Hey, I've got a ringer,
    a swinger
   of a dinger and I'll poke
   like a bloke right up your
  slippy sloppy,
  tight up your flippy floppy.
Let's fuck 'n' never   stop,
fuck until we pop   or drop.
No,   but
    let's   let's
    not
    stop.   Stop.
      Let's
      chat,
       yes,
        let's
        fuck.
  Don't ask me, and I
  won't ask you.
Let's just chat,
  just fuck
   'til we're sore for more.
  Yeah, we'll flood the garden,
   seek no pardon.
We can go on and on, baby,
   on and on.
Let's chat.   Let's fuck.

"Hi, I'm Monique, how can I help you?"

"WOW, MONIQUE, LET'S TALK FUCKING."

Monique is a crimson-dressed shadow. She hasn't a word in her head.

"Rene, Rene?"

Descartes could hear the tenor-player's voice outside in the corridor, but wasn't yet certain whether he'd satisfactorily concluded his experiment with Hélène. He flicked away the mosquito's squashed body, studied what he now acknowledged as the 'relevant digits', and placed them again beneath his nose, pondering for a moment whether he might one day be cast in bronze.

R O D I N ' L L   D O

(it's a cinch)

"Into fields and temples I shall carry the mettle of my soul," Descartes mused, and then he sniffed, a deep, long, philosophical sniff. "Ah," he nodded wistfully, "ah," sniffing again as if to confirm the illumination, "a dead rat, yes, a dead rat."

"Rene? Where the hell are you?"

Descartes licked his fingers, they tasted not of dead rat, but more like salted figs, not that Descartes had ever tasted salted figs, but that's what he thought they would taste like.

"I think Hélène's cunt tastes like salted figs therefore it dœs."

(the mere act of thought was for Descartes proof of the reality of the thought itself)

Then, as if suddenly fearful that time was running out on him, he rammed the relevant digits straight into and up Hélène's arsehole.

Hélène thought of her father's armpits, the old men sitting under the chestnut tree. Hélène thought hard. She thought of the shrine of the Holy Mother which had been constructed on the side of the cart-track halfway between her native village and the city of D****** (which although across the border, was nonetheless the closest city). Needless to say, as a child Hélène had never visited D******, but it had later become her destination, her fate.

"Rene?" this time the tenor-player sounded impatient if not angry, "for God's sake, where are you?"

Descartes wanted to shout 'halfway up Hélène's arsehole', but worried that this might confuse his friend. "I'm here, here in my study."

The tenor-player burst in. He looked agitated. Sweat was pouring from his brow, and his lips appeared engorged and quivering.

Hélène remembered the blue of the Holy Mother's dress, it was the blue of mountain gentians. She remembered the Holy Mother's white head-scarf, remembered her marble flesh and rouged cheeks. She was so pretty. Travellers would leave offerings on the shrine: perfect rounded pebbles, posies of meadow flowers, rabbits' feet, the skulls of crows and ravens, dried bread, crudely modelled clay figurines, corn dollies, the names of the deceased scratched on pieces of blue slate. This was no leper's hole, but Hélène knew now that she too did not belong to that mother. Hélène knew that she was another. Her father had told her. "You are not of us," he had said, "your mother took you in when you were still of the breast. You were taken from your own people that you might be saved, that you too might come to know the Lord, but now we see that it is not possible. You pleasure the boys and laugh when I give warnings. Look, even now you laugh. It is the Devil in you. Hélène, you must leave us, must leave the village. No one knows your secret but your mother and I. Your eyes might betray you, but are there not Spaniards amongst us? Go, Hélène, and never return. You have my blessings, but your mother is too hurt. Goodbye."

"Rene, there you are," exclaimed the tenor-player, so fascinated by Hélène's voluminous breasts that he barely gave a thought to the gravity of his friend's unlikely experiment.

"I am convinced," declared Descartes, overjoyed that he now had an audience, "that the body is no more the mind than the mind is the body."

"In which case," responded the tenor-player, intense as ever, "I think I'll have a handful of this," roughly opening Hélène's coarse cotton blouse and grabbing hold of her tits.

I'd always come back, but you would
always say it again:
"We need to have a little chat."

But who needed to talk when it was no talk at all?
Talk of what? Politics or baby prams?

"WOW, LET'S FUCK TALKING."
(and then I was out again)

Now then, let's see. Oooh, ooh yes, you're a peach.

"Hi, call me Carmen, and I'm yours."

"I want to chat about our relationship."
"Our relationship?"
"Yes."
"Do you mean your relationship with me or my relationship with you?"

"I mean our relationship."

"No, either you mean your idea of your relationship with me or your idea of my relationship with you. Either way, I don't see where ours comes into it."

"So what's the connection?"

"You tell me."

"Oh fuck off."

Now, it doesn't take much to realise that Carmen's lips have had a job done on them: silicon pumped, just like her tits. All the same, I like her tits, and that's enough to get my cock rising unruly and rampant.

I LIKE HER TITS.

"All yours."

"Mmmm, yummy."

The tenor-player looked concerned.

"Rene, there's something I have to ask you."

"Yes, my friend," Descartes responded, revolving his fingers further up Hélène's arsehole, "what do you want to know?"

"What, what is the meaning, the meaning of, of, the blues?" tweaking Hélène's nipples as if to further punctuate his burning desire for a comprehensive answer.

"There, my friend, you have me. I can honestly tell you that I don't know, indeed, I haven't got a clue."

"D-d-don't know?" stuttered the tenor-player, pounding away mindlessly at Hélène's tits like they were lumps of bread-dough, "d-d-don't know. I thought you were a fucking philosopher," completely unable to disguise the dreadful disappointment of the moment, now pummelling away so hard at Hélène's tits that they flapped around like so much wet washing on the line.

"No, but I have struck upon a new theory," mused Descartes, giving the relevant digits what he realised was probably a final and decisive thrust up Hélène's by now somewhat ravaged orifice.

"And what is that?" spluttered the tenor-player, distractedly squeezing and pulling at Hélène's tits as if rather than being delightful mounds of pleasure they had now become some kind of terrible adversary.

"I have struck upon the duality of intent," Descartes announced rather pompously, withdrawing his turd-stained fingers from Hélène's arsehole, "listen to this. I think, but as thought is an act, I also act."

"Is that so?" responded the tenor-player, fumbling with his fly-buttons, pulling aside the saggy cotton of his Y-fronts.

"You don't understand," barked Descartes, involuntarily sucking on his fingers, "mmm, these ain't no figs, but sure as hell they're chicken-licking good."

"Get to the point, Rene," admonished the tenor-player, releasing his steaming erection into the thought-filled air.

"I think therefore I act. What do you make of that?"

"Very little," replied the tenor-player, ramming his cock straight down Hélène's throat, "I don't like the adverb."

"Adverb?" queried Descartes, distractedly stroking Hélène's pussy.

"The therefore," boomed the tenor-player grabbing Hélène by the hair to better control the rhythm of her performance.

"It's a conjunction, you ass."

"It's an adverb."

"A conjunction."

"An adverb."

"Conjunction."

"Adverb."

"Conjunction."

"Adverb."

"Conjunction."

"Adverb."

"Conjunction."

"Adverb."

"Conjunction."

"Adverb."

ALTOGETHER NOW, BOYS.
IN, OUT, IN, OUT,
SHAKE IT ALL ABOUT

"It's a fucking adverb I tell you," screeched the tenor-player, and then, to Hélène, "keep sucking, you bitch," which she did with determined force, "in any case, whatever they are, I've never held with your therefores," wagging his fingers at the now wavering Descartes, "no, Rene, they stink of cheap rationalisation. They're a con, no more than presupposition posing as fact. Ooh, yes, Hélène, that's good, that's good."

"But if I think," grumbled Descartes distractedly, "there must be something that's doing the thinking."

"Maybe it's thought doing the thinking. So, sure you can say I think therefore I think I am, but I'm afraid your clever-arsed one-liner just dœsn't stand up to critical analysis. Keep going, bitch."

Hélène sucked on. She thought of the forest, the village, the menfolk, her father, her journey to D******. And then she was suddenly struck, not by the force of the tenor-player's dick, but by an illumination:

'I am the verb, the doing which is not the word. I who have done am the noun, the word which is not the doing. Either we exist or we merely think therefore we exist. In the former we exist as verb, in the latter we exist as noun. Descartes' 'therefore' merely moves the premise from subject to object and in so doing shifts us from the doing to the done.

If existence precedes essence, existence must be essence, just as if essence depends on existence, essence must be existence. What do these silly men think they're thinking about?'

"No more therefores," Descartes muttered dolefully, a tear forming in his icy cold, blue eyes, running down his cheek and splashing onto Hélène's horse-like thighs.

"I'm sorry to upset you, Rene," consoled the tenor-player, "but how about I think I am? It's neat and no one can pick holes in it."

"I think I am. Mmm, it's a possibility," Descartes whispered half to himself, half to Hélène's quivering arse, "mmm, I think ..." solemnly rising from his desk, "I think I act, mmm, yes, yes" rushing towards the open window and diving headlong into the raging storm that carries him still. It carries him as leaf. It carries him as feather. It carries him as discarded thought. It carries him as ether. It carries him as a pair of shiny red satin panties, cast like a symphony of form in search of essence.

"Jeez, Hélène," sighed the tenor-player, "I was beginning to think we'd never get rid of the old bastard. Now, tell me, do *you* know the meaning of the blues? Do you?" shooting his load in one mighty gush past Hélène's tonsils.

Hélène slowly withdrew the tenor-player's cock from her mouth and vomited all over Descartes' desk.

"CHAT. WE NEED TO CHAT."

"Okay, I'll chat. I'll tell of how you turned your back on me, how you stirred your coffee when I wanted the spoon, how you played with yourself when I wanted to expound. EXPOUND. I wanted to expound. If you had listened then, you wouldn't be asking now. I WANTED TO EXPOUND."

"EXPOUND OR EXPAND?"
"Fuck You."
"Let's chat about it."

YOU PLAYED WITH YOURSELF
and, what's more,
I'VE NEVER LIKED CONFERENCE PEARS.

THE SEVEN PILLARS FOUND

†

1
NAUGHTY NURSE.
RED HAIR, NURSE UNIFORM, STIMULATOR, STETHOSCOPE.

2
DOUBLE SCOOPS TITTY FUCK.
GET YOURSELF BETWEEN THESE BOUNCING BOOBS.
WITH LUBRICANT.

3
SMART ASS.
SHE LIKES IT FROM BEHIND, BUT LOVES IT ANY WAY.
TWO REALISTIC VIBRATING HOLES.

4
VINYL DOLLY BUSTER.
SHE'S NAUGHTY, SHE'S NICE, SHE'S YOURS, SHE VIBRATES.
SHE HAS THREE HOLES.

5
SUPER FANTASY.
REAL FEEL SKIN. WIDE MOUTH. DEEP THROAT.
WHIP, HANDCUFFS, LUBE, VIBRATING PUSSY AND BUM.

6
PUSSY AND ASS.
FULL SIZE CAST OF BUM. DO YOUR PRESS-UPS
WITH THIS, YOU WON'T LAST FIVE MINUTES.
TWO REAL FEEL LOVING HOLES.

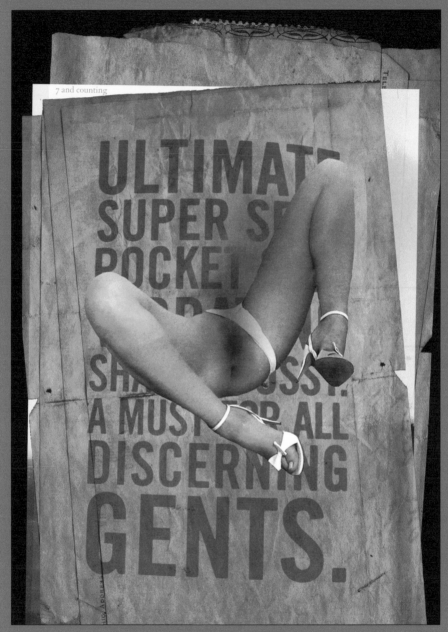

7 and counting

ULTIMATE
SUPER S
POCKE

SH   SSY.
A MUST OR ALL
DISCERNING
GENTS.

The Rejection is an extract from *This Crippled Flesh – A Book of Philosophy And Filth*
by Penny Rimbaud · Illustrated by Alice Smith

Sarah Janes'
SEX DREAM DIARY

WHAT FOLLOWS IS A COLLECTION OF DREAMS I HAVE written down over the last couple of years. Seeing as it is the *Idler*'s sex issue, most of them have a bit of sex in. They are written in a pretty simple way because I have written them upon waking whilst the dream is still fresh in my memory.

I sometimes wonder whether dreams are interesting for anyone other than the dreamer, but I truly think dream lives are as meaningful as those so-called 'real-lives' we are supposedly living and having now just read through all the of below I can see how incredible, life-changing and instructive they are. I can see codes and predictions in them. I've been meaning to put this collection together for a while. I spoke to Tom about writing this piece quite a few months ago but emotionally these past couple of years have been a difficult and confusing time and it seemed up until the last dream, I wasn't quite at the stage I wanted to be at. For me these dreams document a love affair, a broken heart and its total resurrection and now that the cycle is complete I can happily present it.

The real life that ran parallel to this dream life can be summed up thus: fell in love with best friend who had girlfriend, he fell in love with me but moved away to foreign climes whilst promising to return for me. When he returned he still couldn't break away from his girlfriend, she found out he cheated on her, much heartache ensued, my faith in true love was destroyed, I broke away from him, became all spiritual, had a dance party for New Years Eve with my favourite people in the world and slowly realised that I could be happy without him, then one night — the night of the last dream recorded here — I spent the night with somebody else and I felt utterly complete and satisfied and happy and in love and liberated from my broken heart.

On the subject of sex, I do believe that the true sexual self is the true self and the ability to express your true self physically and emotionally through sex is one of the key elements to a happy existence.

MONDAY, AUGUST 15, 2005

Last night I dreamt there was a Terminator loose in the world. I don't think he was after me but he was after somebody I knew. I was with my true love, not sure who that is yet, and we were running and running and there were big black pumas and wild dogs after us and they were all possessed by the Terminator and they all wanted blood.

We ran and ran and went through many exotic and beautiful lands and ancient buildings and then finally we found a pretty spot, a painted beach hut in a happy place that the Terminator didn't know about. I guess there was a chance that he might of found us one day but I looked into my true love's eyes and I felt completely happy and in love and knew that I wanted to be with him forever. We held hands and walked towards our beach hut, it was painted blue and there was a garden in front with a fountain.

We found a heart-shaped purse on the floor. It was heavy. We looked at it for a moment and he weighed it in his hand and said that there wasn't any money in it. The purse was two hearts together, one pink and one red and it was wet, looked like it had been in a storm or the sea. We walked over the threshold of our beach hut and at the same time realised there was money and we were going back to get it, because with money we would really survive, we would make dinner and sit outside our beach hut as the sun set and look at the fountain and be happy, far away from the Terminator and the black pumas.

WEDNESDAY, AUGUST 31, 2005
Wet Dreams?

I had the most fantastic dream the other night. It was the night when Mars was really bright in the sky. I dreamt I was standing on the earth looking at the most enormous full moon and the surface of the earth was a reflection upon it. It was the most beautiful luminous vision. The moon took up half the sky and I could feel the curve of the earth under my feet.

Then I was on a huge steamboat sailing around the world. I was on the deck in a double bed with my ex boyfriend. All of our friends were on board too but we were alone in the fresh air. The boat glided very fast through the water and seemed to be able to move very quickly around all obstacles, of which there were many, many other huge liners and the like.

As we approached the coast of Finland my ex started trying to bring me off with his thumb in a very matter of fact kind of a way. The duvet cover was red checks, I was very excited but he was just a little off the mark, for some time I was agonising just to the right and finally I finished myself off and reached the most fantastic climax. Then I woke up in a throbbing sweat.

I have been asking my friends about wet dreams and they say they are rare. The boys don't seem any better off than the girls. I thought it was a very precious treat and I'm devising some method of cultivating the ability. I reckon magnets at the back of the head and the sound of waves to encourage theta waves in the brain might be a start.

MONDAY, 5 SEPTEMBER, 2005

I had this horrible dream the other night whereby I was going out with my own dad. I didn't want to but he insisted. So we was getting it on when I suddenly comes over all repulsed because it must be said he wasn't too shit hot in the sack and he didn't have the necessary precautionary equipment so I run out into a public toilet in my pants and a vest and in this public toilet a little group of old ladies starting interviewing me about why I was crying. I said, I used to be married to this chap and it ended and I started dating his ex-father-in-law. They put two and two together and quickly surmised that I was diddling me own pops. Disgust ensued and I woke up trying desperately to forget. It was one of those, don't remember...don't remember, what am I not remembering again? Oh shit!

TUESDAY, 11 OCTOBER, 2005
Myth of Dead Horse and Girl in the Rapids

I have a theory that when you are in pain your dreams seem more real. None of my brain books have borne this out of yet but I am sure I am right. Do you think you need a maths GCSE in order to study neurology? You've got to count and multiply stuff. Anyway.

I had a beautiful dream whilst I was suffering from the womb ache. It looked like a myth, like a series of moving oil paintings. There was a young girl riding a horse, I was partly within the young girl and partly watching, She and the horse fell, or were hit by a falling tree and they were both killed, I felt the air empty from my lungs. Then the two of them were put on a wooden raft and floated down a tempestuous river that led to the underworld. Their bodies were decorated with flowers and the dead horse had its limbs arranged so that it looked like it was comfortably lying down and the girl was lying at the horse's side.

Suddenly I realised that I and she didn't want to die and we took a sharp intake of breath and came back to life, the petals falling from our eyes and splashing water fresh on our face. The river made itself into a small horse-shape, which we climbed onto. The watery horse fought against the rapids and we made it to the shore and hence life and the watery horse returned to the rapids. The real horse was now alone on its raft to death.

WEDNESDAY, 16 DECEMBER, 2005
End of The World Whale

I was living in a tree house with a group of women and they were sort of making me over for some special event. One of the women had a glider and she took me out in it. We glided all over the city, which was the beautiful Gothic Eastern European type city, maybe Gdansk.

We flew over a harbour, catching the sea breeze and across the mouth of the river whereby I spotted a HUGE shark's fin sticking out of the water. It was really huge, the size of a car. I pointed it out to the woman I was with and we followed it along the river, which wound through the beautiful city, under bridges and around church spires. We lost sight of the shark's fin and set the glider down at the end of a brick tunnel. The walls were wet and it looked sort of like a sewer, this town was also a bit like Vienna in the Third Man. I say to the women, 'if we run to the end of the tunnel we will probably catch up with the shark, it'll be about here now.'

I could tell that she didn't think it was likely but we ran to the end of the tunnel anyway and sure enough at the end of the tunnel was an industrial canal with walkways either side and a brick wall opposite us. As we got close to the canal side, the shark's fin drew level with us. A crowd of people gathered to watch. We all held our breath as the huge shark's fin stopped. Slowly it emerged from the water and the crowd were scared but finally it revealed itself to be a beautiful whale and everyone sighed with relief. Then however, its huge form — it took up the whole river- transmuted into a demon black whale with a big round mouth full of sharp teeth and it was telling us that it was the end of the world and that we were all going to die, that it was going to GET all of us. This was quite frightening, especially when a kind of holographic image of the devil's face was projected onto the brick wall opposite, I felt as though I was really seeing the devil and it was quite scary because I never thought the devil existed. The devil was saying that it was the end of the world as well and I ran back down the tunnel and realised that I wanted to go somewhere to find someone to say goodbye.

I looked at a map and I searched on the internet to find this person. The internet said it was the first day of snow where they were. Then I looked at the map and the map became real and was covered in snow and then next thing, I was really there. The map only showed a car park by the sea, but really it was a beautiful city full of huge cream houses, with burning lanterns outside. I walked along the streets and realised that the city planners had a thing for using wild and exotic animals for urban display. Like we might have a floral clock on a roundabout or hanging baskets, along their streets there were sad looking animals in small cages, stacked up in architecturally interesting ways, there were monkeys, maybe lions and tigers but certainly the most significant of these was a stack of elephants. There were three elephants chained to very small round, barred platforms all balanced precariously on top of one another. They were chained so close to the bars that they couldn't move at all and they wanted desperately to be free.

There was a particularly wild spirited one at the bottom and he was wrangling furiously against his chain so that eventually he freed his head but the fierceness of his movements set the whole stack of platforms tumbling and the structure toppled like a collapsing ferris wheel across the road. I looked away because I didn't want to see the elephants get crushed and when I turned back I was talking to an intellectual grey haired woman who looked like she bought her clothes from Hampstead Bazaar, about whether or not she thought it was cruel that the city planners liked to use wild animals in their urban displays. She said that she just wanted to keep the animals alive. I wanted them to be free but I couldn't decide whether it would be better to live in captivity or be dead.

SATURDAY, 13 MAY, 2006
True Love Underground, Sarah Janes: Film Star …

A man appeared inside my head. I was quite old and reflecting upon my life. He whispered — 'I am your first true love, remember all the good times we had?' I was standing in a queue, I didn't remember him at all but he told me all about our old life together, we used to visit a Turkish bar near Elephant and Castle he said, we first kissed underground in the sewers. He would take me to the spot and show me the neon sign he left — I think his name was Vik. He kissed me from inside of my brain and this was very strange and half way through I realised I was actually kissing four chair legs and everyone in the queue I was in started looking at me peculiarly. Then the man himself came to take me by the hand. He morphed in and out of people that I know and don't know. At one point he was a beautiful Turkish woman and then someone else and then someone else. I felt that I did truly love him though and as he lead me through, what he said were familiar streets, I did actually start to remember.

We went underground into the tunnels of the sewers. The walls were painted white. A river ran fast below a railing. We were now surrounded by my friends and he knelt down and felt a patch of wall which soon revealed our names engraved but painted over with the thick white paint and there was a golden rosette — like the ones you use when wrapping presents and there was a neon sign filled with green glitter — that spelled our names inside a circle. The idea was that we would kiss down here where we first kissed and it would be magical.

I had now returned to my youthful state, walking backwards through time to this underground sewer. Our friends were pulling us along and I had to make them leave so that we could have a moment alone.

We leant against the railing with the rushing river below and finally I looked into his eyes and knew who he was. As he leant forwards to kiss me and I to him, he slipped and fell over the railing, taking another woman with him — she was the secretary that looked after the tourist sewer trips, she said his name, she said she had worked for his father, I jumped in to save him, he was hanging just above the river and I reached out for him but his legs came away in my hands and he was gone.

Then the water turned into maybe a foot deep and bubbly bath water and I was with my little nephews giving them a bath. George was old enough for me to have a proper conversation with. He screamed in agony when I splashed cold water on him, they said I was being too rough, I kept throwing them about and dipping their heads under the water, then finally I flung them out of the bath and they towelled themselves dry.

Someone told me that they had made a film of my life, only it was set in wartime Britain and Bexhill, my name was being touted and printed all over the place and people could not distinguish between the actress Sarah Janes and the real Sarah Janes.

Sunday, 14 May, 2006
White Naked Cretan Dolphin, Crazy Hoopoes, Evil Friends

I was lost in a big house, searching rooms. There was a ceiling-less room in the garden. The landlords had not finished putting the glass in so there was a wispy net in its place. A beautiful house and a small tree in the gardens, jays and hoopoes, first one and then many — huge versions of hoopoes that wouldn't put their crest up unless they felt happy. I am delighted to see them but my friends are taunting them, making them screech but the birds don't fly away. My friends are rubbing their faces against their beaks, pulling their wings and feathers. They are the guardians of my dreams. I try to protect them but they don't fly away.

I am a dog, talking to the house owner's children, New Age parents giving them no freedom, the girl drawing sketches of their diet and regime, they're given supplements in their sleep, they are given children's sleep programmes to influence their dreams, games to play, exhausting, unimaginative, trapped in a blue cartoon. They only feel free when they are allowed to eat their breakfast in the garden. Waiting for a killer whale, feeling nervous in a lake in Crete but instead a pod of dolphins. Me in the water, my friend too scared to join in. 'Look at me'. The white isle holiday advertisement, best time to go July. Women are wandering naked into the ocean.

Wednesday, 6 September, 2006
Katrina … Garrotted Porky Pig … Lobster Claw in Assassin's Pussy

I just woke up from the most interesting dream. I was on an airplane upon which there was a conference for children as to the effects of hurricane Katrina — their logo was a garrotted Porky Pig. Someone gave me a camera and asked me to film it, then I went to find the pilot but he had been overpowered by a charismatic clairvoyant who told me that a naked African lady assassin was about to make an attempt on her life and force her down into the sea. The naked female assassin came and from behind I forced a huge detached lobster claw into her pussy, followed by a wedge of lemon, which deterred her from her course — she said I beat her fair and square and gave me the lobster claw as a prize. I cracked the lobster claw open and it was full of tiny blue balls.

SATURDAY, 9 SEPTEMBER, 2006
More little balls . . . Back Damage . . . Brain Bingo
. . . True Love in a Limo . . . PAN numbers

I had this really weird dream that I went to a festival and there was this band playing that everybody worshipped like gods. I didn't think they'd be that impressive but when I stood by the stage I felt like I had entered some new and incredibly beautiful level of existence. People covered themselves in war paint and sacrificed themselves on stage and it was a big thing to appear on stage next to them, people came in costume and fell at their feet crying blood.

There was one attempt to get on stage that ended in semi-disaster. Someone swung down onto the stage from a big chain hanging from the rafters. He smashed into the bass player who fell on the floor and promptly started screaming having done something terrible to his back. The perpetrator of the crime was mortified and everyone felt almost as sorry for him as they did for the bass player — whose name I forget (it might of been something like Gareth).

Anyway, cue two extremely beautiful Thai nurses still powdering their noses, coming over to the rescue. They sit on top of him and I look horrified as they manipulate his back and it seems to crack and splinter in their brutal but well-manicured hands. They fold him up like a little parcel and push him into the back of an ambulance-style limousine. I am instructed to accompany him to St. Mary's hospital, suite number 76. This is written on a plastic wristband.

In the ambulance/limo I stroke his hair, he has a bald patch at the back of his head and his pain can only be allayed by me stroking it in circular movements whilst he strokes my legs. He moans and groans through his mixture of pleasure and pain and I derive some pleasure from our peculiar situation also.

We arrive at St. Mary's and tell the driver we need suite 76. In suite 76 we find ourselves immediately seen by a genius doctor with a Swiss accent. He sits the patient on the counter and fits a little plug into the small of his back. He blows air into his spine and tiny green bubble-balls flow out of the little plug and slip across the steel table he's sitting on top of.

We look at each other utterly baffled and the doctor explains that his back is back to normal, in fact, it's even better than before and along the way the doctor has also discovered that something amazing has happened to his brain which means that it has the ability of developing at a new rate, doubling, tripling its power and increasing its PAN number. The PAN number somehow translates as — neurological capability and is broken down into units. Delighted with this news the patient is filled with a new enthusiasm and somehow his brain bingo has affected me also and there is a sense of many great adventures about to be taken ...

TUESDAY, 12 SEPTEMBER, 2006
Smashed Baby Alligators ... Free Trip to Hawaii

I dreamt that we were in this porn king's casino in a castle and we were playing one of those 2p machines that was done up like a fancy blackjack table. Anyways you put your 2p in and it pushes a bunch of stuff out my side. The stuff is mainly the smashed limbs and heads of a collection of baby alligators but there is also a ticket for seven free tickets for a holiday to Hawaii. Worth £782 apiece! I am understandably cock-a-hoop and ready to fetch me lei and grass skirt but everyone else seems to doubt the validity of the tickets and can't be bothered. This frustrates me enormously and I end up having to go back to my hotel and round up strangers. Pfff!

TUESDAY, 19 SEPTEMBER, 2006
Sex with a Dead Friend ...

Last night I dreamt that I had sex with a friend of mine who died a few years ago. I have not thought about him for a while and it was very realistic and amazing and it got me to thinking that maybe if there is an afterlife it involves swanning around in other people's dreams and having sex with them. What a fucking hoot! Please, let it be true!!

SUNDAY, 3 DECEMBER, 2006

This is the dream ... In so-called 'real-life' I'm going through the same old rigmarole, a couple of highly intense, passionate and fun filled days followed by the usual fake emotion, rehearsed blubbering, vows to change, a swift departure, some dramatic statements, the last one of mine being — 'I feel like you have killed me'. Then the decision that this time I would like to fight it out with proper fisticuffs but each punch is feeble and my attempts to grab hold of his hair and smack his face into the floor end up with me just thinking that actually, I don't really want to hurt him.

He has this stack of feeble gifts for his return journey, a bunch of fake flowers, a petrol can, something else made of cardboard and something else.

His face turns into mine and then suddenly I regain my strength and am able to hit myself quite forcefully and get a kick out of it and evidently that face of me that is getting hit is getting a kick out of it too. We are both on our knees and in my red pyjamas and every time I hit myself I come crawling back for more and my annoying face all flushed from punches invites another slap and then my face reverts to his for a moment and takes some stinging backhanders but then it's back to me and I realise that if this is a dream and I can do anything I want then I would rather fuck myself than beat myself up — BRILLIANT dream logic! So I draw my hips towards me and start unbuttoning my pyjama top and it becomes quite erotic, but my heart starts bleeding and I realise that my family are all in the room and I hear my dad say that I'm going to have to take back all those new clothes he bought me because life isn't going quite according to plan. My red pyjamas have turned into the white new clothes he was talking about and now there is a big red stain at the heart and they are ruined.

HA! Now this sounds like a bad dream but no not really, dreams are all about the way you feel and I feel good about this dream.

SUNDAY, 10 DECEMBER, 2006

Yesterday I prayed to David Bowie for guidance and this — NO WORD OF an EFFIN! LIE — is what goes and happens! I got some magic tea from Amanda, drank it round Gayle's and dreamt that I met David Bowie in New Orleans. This was the story... I had committed a serious crime in my youth. I was in a little gang that broke into a big government building and we wrecked it, smashed it up and stole money and there was a police cordon around the whole building but because they didn't expect the culprits to be kids we got away with it and just mingled in with the crowd. However, the cops had kind of been after us the whole time and so me and my friend Jennie (who was in the gang) moved to New Orleans, Jennie was the only one of us who had made any money off the venture and she opened a little boutique on Magazine Street and then she spent lots of money on a very beautiful necklace that everybody could see was very expensive (*Goodfellas*-style). A girl that worked in a shop a couple of doors down said that Jennie shouldn't go around flouting such obviously expensive jewellery because some people might guess where she got the money from and as it happens this girl had been at the scene of the crime all those years ago and was going to grass us up to the pigs so we had to go on the run again or at least lay low.

So cue David Bowie coming to town in a jeep and I am his guide, he is very careful with money and he's on the phone to his dad who wants Bowie to buy him a mobile phone and David Bowie is trying to ensure that whilst he's prepared to pay for it, he wants to pay a fair price and not get ripped off. He says to his dad, do some research find out what one you really want and I'll pay for it. At first I am sort of surprised and think that he is a bit tight but after a while I realise he is merely setting an example for me and that his guidance is for me to be careful with money! Excellent and timely wisdom and not the sort of advice I thought I needed but actually the only kind of advice I ever need.

So me and Bowie are driving around New Orleans and it is truly magical, I am showing him the sights and we are avoiding murder scenes of which there are many and we walk through one particularly distressing one where there is still lots of blood on the ground and I leave my footprints in it and worry that maybe the police might be able to track me down for my past crime but I definitely feel safe and protected with Bowie and after a while we get back in his jeep and we drive to a beautiful field and into the longest grass and have a little sleep hidden by the tall grass. What a PERFECT DREAM!!!

FRIDAY, 22 DECEMBER, 2006
AMAZING Red Squirrel Psychic Dream ...

I had an AMAZING lucid dream about meeting a red squirrel and it being able to talk and being psychic and it telling me I'd have amazing sexual chemistry with a Sagittarian. It knew everything about me (which I suppose makes a lot of sense) but now I can't remember exactly what my future holds, which is probably for the best. It had a very cute old lady voice and everybody loved it. Even though it was the dream world and lions and tigers and pangolins and whales live therein, I remember being really amazed by seeing a red squirrel as I walked down the street, but the DOUBLE-WHAMMY was that it could talk and extra bonus tell me my future.

Fan-tas-tic!

All Hail the Monkey Moon 2080 days left, Light-Bearing Dreams!

Last night I dreamt that I was initiated into Basque culture by doing a special dance on a sandy beach late at night in traditional Basque costume which featured a long veil that the wind drew over the sea. It was very spiritual and beautiful and the long black veil made elegant lines in the breeze across the waves. A man played guitar but I danced alone. The dance went on for seemingly hours and at one point I felt self-conscious and suddenly this transparent circle of energy appeared to me from the sea, picked me up, lifted me high above the ocean, everything was deep blue, I was really scared that I was going to drown but then I started to enjoy the feeling of flying and I remember feeling that I should just enjoy this moment. A while later, the energy deposited me gently in the sea. The sea was calm and soothing and I was part of it and I started singing the theme to the *Third Man*. Then someone told me the phosphorous was running out, or maybe they said Bosphorous — which is an ancient kingdom of Greece. Phosphorous means light-bearer.

Ode to the Deep Sea

Dark depths of mystery,
Ancient and true,
Nimble consciousness,
In the creature soup,
Energy and light,
Light made matter,
Waves rise and fall,
Atoms rotate,
Kinesis directs,
Evolution shapes,
Under this life,
Pulsates another.

WEDNESDAY, 24 JANUARY, 2007
C ... c ... c ... cold ... Snow ... Dildo Milk Dreams ... Pouncing Cat

Yippppppeeee, today it snowed! This always marks a real shift in emotions and me getting a cold. I got a cold I think from when I stayed over Wendy's and her cat wouldn't stop pouncing all over me in the middle of the night. Then furthermore, when at approximately 9am I did manage to have several seconds of shut-eye, I dreamt that I was with my mum and dad who were making out in their underwear in Wendy's kitchen, whilst cooking an enormous pan of meat and then my dad made them both a cup of tea and I was alarmed to discover that he was squirting the milk, for said tea, out a milk-filled rubber dildo dangling from a string round his waist. Bluergh! That's enough to wake anyone up. Wendy told me that they were making her feel sick and I agreed.

MONDAY, 26 MARCH, 2007

The night before last I had the most incredible dream that I was living in a house that was built in the trenches of the First World War. I was given some heroin, which in real life I have never tried and it was the most incredible sensation. There were white fireworks exploding in my heart that I could see and feel. I tried to move my face but it was like a mask but telepathically I was communicating with someone or thing. I could feel the chemicals sparkling in my brain and bloodstream and I felt liberated and full of love. Then somebody knocked on the door and it was the person I love and he told me that I would have to move out of the house because the whole area was about to be reclaimed by the sea. Either before or after this, a couple had invited me to an orgy. Initially I declined, but eventually they twisted my arm.

SHE BROUGHT THE VASELINE

A short story by Mark Manning

'WHAT?' SAID KIRKY, A LOOK OF HORROR ON HIS FACE AS IF I'd just told him that I was a man of the arse. 'Yeah man, in her handbag, one of those big jars as well,' I replied, amused at his utter revulsion.

'The dirty fucking cow. I'm well fucking shut of her then, aren't I? The fucking slag,' spat my friend.

Carved in stone at the oracle in Delphi there were two precepts: '*Know thyself*' and '*Nothing to excess*'.

I believe that up there with those eternal truths there should have been another: '*Never shag your mate's missus.*'

My worst friend, Kirky, and his missus were having a party.

My main crush of all time was going to be there.

I'd rehearsed my seduction like a particularly unpleasant General, practised a million chat up lines in front of a mirror, scrubbed my balls so clean you could eat your dinner off of them.

Groovy black flares and a Black Sabbath t-shirt.

'Tonight Julie Cunningham, you will be mine,' I said to my reflection.

Like a cockney werewolf: *my hair was perfect*.

I bought a party seven and made my way to the party.

I couldn't get her off my mind.

Another timeless truth unfortunately however, is that a young man's brain is in his dick.

Hence the dreadful mistake I made that evening.

The party got into full barf.

A typical 1970s teenage cider job: kids honking up everywhere, lots of necking and love biting, menthol fags, fighting and crackly T Rex records distorting in Dansette mono.

But where was Julie? I hadn't seen her for ages, please God don't let her have gone home.

The bog was upstairs.

I negotiated my way up there, avoiding the vomit, which seemed to be everywhere, and there she was.

Snogging Kirky outside the shitter.

Bad.

Not good.

I was devastated, what the fuck did he think he was doing, swapping spit with the girl of my dreams?

The bastard, he knew how keen I was on her.

I could see their shiny tongues like pink snakes; it looked like he was eating her face.

I felt sick.

I have made gazillions of mistakes in my life.

In fact, when I think about it, my entire life often seems like one giant mistake.

But there on that landing at the teenage cider party I decided to make probably the dumbest fucking mistake of my entire life.

I decided out of some twisted loop of teenage logic to go back downstairs and fuck his missus.

She was pissed as a cunt, so it wasn't difficult.

I manoeuvered her into the back yard and did her over the dustbins. Just as I jizzed all over her arse and up the back of her sparkly top she chucked up big-time, all down the back of the bins: carrots, cider, everything.

Horrible.

What the fuck did Kirky see in her?

I wiped my dick on her hair and went back inside to the teenage rampage feeling justified.

That would teach the disloyal fucker.

I noticed Kirky, who had now disentangled himself from that filthy whore upstairs, noticing me coming back into the house from the back door.

I didn't say anything, just grabbed another can of Skol lager and decked it in one, trying to drown the guilt that was already creeping up on me like a scabby farm cat with three legs.

But what the fuck? He'd been all over my Julie, the bastard.

I split when I saw him going out of the back door into the yard.

I'd left his lovely girlfriend covered in spunk with her knickers round her ankles puking her ring down the back of the bins.

I didn't really want to be there when he found her.

There was no way I was going to be able to talk my way out of that one.

The next morning I was laying in bed wanking over Julie, I'd forgiven her already, the slag, when I heard a timid knock on the back door.

I peered through the curtains. It was Kirky's missus.

With a black eye.

Shit, what the fuck did she want?

I let her in. 'He knows,' she said

'Well, I kind of guessed that,' I replied, nodding at her shiner.

'Do you want to go to Blackpool for a few days?' she blurted, feeling my knob through my jeans.

I like Blackpool, I always have. It's got a great funfair with loads of wooden rollercoasters and stuff. 'What, now?' I answered, already thinking about all the great rides and flashing lights.

'Yeah, look, I've taken all the money out of our joint bank account,' she opened her handbag: it was stuffed with fivers and tenners and a big jar of Vaseline.

'What's the Vaseline for?' I said, intrigued.

'So you can fuck my arse with it,' she said, a wicked smirk curling itself around her face.

'All right then,' I said already imagining buggering her on a wooden rollercoaster high above the pleasure beach.

'How did he find out?' I said on the 11.10 to Blackpool.

'Well, I know he's a bit thick, you know,' she said, lighting a fag. 'But when he came out and found me lying on the floor, covered in spunk with my knickers round my ankles … well, it must have been pretty obvious, even to him.'

'Do you know that some of the rollercoasters in Blackpool are listed buildings?' I said, not wanting to think about the unforgivable sin I had committed and the ones I was about to commit.

The next three days were a whirlwind of rollercoasters, alcohol and buggery.

We were holed up in some little seaside b & b. Kirky's missus wiped the sperm off of her face and looked thoughtful. 'Maybe I should call my mother, see what's happening back home, they might be worried about me?' said Blackpool's cock-sucker of the year.

She went downstairs to the payphone while I poured myself a refreshing 9am vodka and orange.

I'd been pretty much totally pissed for the previous three days so obviously I hadn't given a thought about anything that wasn't happening in the present.

I'd been quite happy shagging the arse off of Kirky's missus and riding around all day on wooden rollercoasters.

Totally forgotten about school and Kirky, my parents and everything. But that was all about to change any second.

Her face was ashen. 'He's in hospital,' she said. 'Tried to kill himself with an overdose of junior disprin.'

'Shit' seemed appropriate.

'The bastard couldn't even do that right,' she laughed, the heartless slut.

We decided to go and face the shit hitting the fan.

Well, *she* did. I just kept my head down for a few weeks, I'd heard rumours that my ex worst friend was carrying a knife and was going to kill me.

I opened my door one afternoon and shat a brick: it was Kirky. 'Do you fancy a pint?' he said breezily. 'The bitch has gone off with a fucking pikey,' he continued. There were loads of pikeys in Leeds. Horrible, thieving bastards they were, that couldn't read. 'He can fucking have her,' he added.

It was if nothing had happened. 'Are we still mates then?' I asked tentatively.

'Course we fucking are,' he replied nonchalantly. 'I'm not falling out over some stupid fucking woman.'

I got the first round in and relaxed my sphincter.

'Paddy Murphy, he's called,' said my friend. We both laughed. 'Paddy *fucking* Murphy, do you think he's Irish?'

SEE THIS SHED ?
IT'S FULL OF SHIT !

SEE THIS HOUSE ?
IT'S FULL OF RATS !
THEY FUCKING LIVE THERE !

Lea d' Asco by Lindsay Brunnock

IDLE
PUR
SUITS

How to
MEASURE THINGS

Warwick Cairns throws away the ruler

¶ Let's say that you need to measure some stuff, right now.
Right now, let's say that you have to know the size or the weight
of ... Oh, I don't know — this magazine, say. Don't ask me why —
just say you have to. ¶ Before you start, you need to ask yourself
this: can I really be arsed to do this thing properly right now?
¶ If you can, you'll need to go off now and get some things: a ruler,
some scales, a life, and so on. ¶ But if you can't, then you're what
is known as 'normal,' and this article is for you. ¶ Most of us, most
of the time, have better things to think about. There's always a
strong temptation to bodge and guess when it comes to measuring,
and to rely on rules of thumb that sort of get us to roughly what
we want to know. This has always been so, all around the world;
and because it has, every country has ended up with what are
known as 'traditional measures' — which, mostly, are the 'rules-of-
thumb' that have 'stuck': the ones that have worked well enough
for long enough by generations of normal people who can't be
bothered to do it 'properly'. ¶ Let's start with a thumb-sized rule,
to show you what I mean. Put your thumb down flat, make a mark
either side of your knuckle, and, for an average-sized male hand,
what you've got is what most cultures call a 'thumb' (or pouce,
dum, or pulgada) but which we call an inch. Most countries use
inch-diameter plumbing: you can stick your thumb down the hole
to stop the water. ¶ Going a bit bigger, put your hand down flat,
mark the width at the widest part, where your thumb joins, and
what you have is a hand, or four inches. You can use it to 'walk' up
the legs of your livestock, if you have any, or else up your walls to
work out where to knock nails in — especially in America, where
the wooden studs behind the plaster are four hands apart.
¶ Bigger still, if you take off your shoe, you'll find that the width
of your hand fits into the length of it three times — which makes

twelve inches. And if your feet are average size (75% of men take an 8, 9 or 10) then the sole of your shoe will be pretty much the same size as the 'official' foot (or pied or fuss, or even kanejaku). You can use it to pace out a room, or a field. If you're a woman, you'll need leave a slight gap between your steps: for small feet — size five, say — leave two thumbs' width, and for size sevens leave just one. ¶ You can weigh stuff, too, without equipment. Just hold something you know the weight of in one hand, and something else in the other. For the thing you know the weight of, try a nice smooth stone that fills the palm of your hand snugly so that your fingers curl around but don't quite touch. Or else some fruit — a handful of apples, say. Either way you'll be holding roughly a pound (or livre or pfund). Pounds vary a little from culture to culture, but not by nearly as much as you might think; and no-one at all seems to have gone anywhere near as big as the kilogramme — apart from the metric system, that is. If you want to know why this should be, try picking up a kilogramme of loose apples without dropping any. Using both hands doesn't make it any easier, either. ¶ Volume: a comfortable mouthful of liquid will roughly fill an espresso-cup. Half of that is a fluid ounce. You can fit more in, but it starts to hurt at the back of your throat. A really painfully-full mouthful is half a cup, one average-sized glass of wine, or four ounces. Four of these make a US pint, and five make a UK pint. ¶ But if you offer people drinks measured out like this they tend, I find, to run away. There's a lesson in that, even: if they sprint, flat out, there comes a point where they can't keep it up any longer and either slow down or collapse. If you follow them, sharpish, with a tape-measure, you'll note that this distance is an eighth of a mile. This, as it happens, is a furlong, the distance the ancient Romans called a stadium and used for their running-tracks. ¶ So next time someone asks you to measure something, it's a simple choice: either get off your backside and fetch a ruler, or end up gasping by the roadside in a pool of your own vomit, pursued by a nutter waving a pint-glass in one hand and a tape-measure in the other. 🐌

How to
GO EXTREME RAMBLING

Don't fence me in, says Robert Twigger

¶ The Exteme Ramblers Association (ERA) is Britain's smallest walking organisation. It has no celebrities such as Floella Benjamin to boost its profile. There are no local groups to join. However, it answers a real need: the right to ramble without feeling bored, hemmed in and constricted by unnecessary rules.

¶ The Extreme Ramblers association was not my idea. My friend, Ben Forster, an Australian, was one day exclaiming on what a great word 'rambling' was. It seems that in Oz they have no sense of the word rambling being associated with dull folks in sensible footwear and cagoules tramping along well worn paths. For Ben 'rambling' conjured up a world of easy pleasure, the tortoise taking a nap alongside the hare, exploration on a fascinating micro-scale, enjoyment of England in the magical time of May and early June.

¶ I quickly disabused him. Seeing that 'rambling' had been 'taken' (like an internet domain name) he suggested Extreme Rambling as a return to all that was good and true about rambling, and so the ERA was born.

¶ We realized we would need our own country code — since breaking the country code was something all true ramblers take pleasure in from time to time. Our ERA country code is as follows:

¶ The Extreme Rambler Country Code

1. The electric fence challenge: approach the electric fence with a stalk of grass. Gradually shorten the distance until you touch for a second the fence. Increase the duration of holding. The person who can hold the fence the longest is the winner.
2. Vault that five bar gate: all gates should be vaulted. Knackered gates are easier as they are nearer the ground.
3. Brolly folly: try rambling with a brolly instead of a cagoule, mac, or waterproof of any kind.
4. Take home other people's litter: go on, dare you.

5. Cross fields with bulls in if only by the corner. You will feel good in the pub later.
6. Right to roam. You have a right to roam everywhere. Some people may dispute this. Only one way to find out though.
7. Be expert at ducking between strands of barbed wire.
8. Be able to start a fire with a single match, a tissue and a kitkat wrapper and brew nettle tea in an old coke can.
9. Drink water from crystal clear mountain streams and talk for the rest of the day about dead sheep.
10. Throw giant sticky burrs at your fellow walkers in a spirit of companionable fun.
11. Only do the above if it appeals to you. Extreme rambling is about escaping rules not making them.

Extreme Rambling puts the challenge back into rambling.
A few new challenges include:

¶ Urban Silva. Use your silva compass (or any compass) to walk across a part of London (or any big city) you don't know to a designated location (pub, coffeshop) no A-Z or GPS allowed.
¶ Wader Walk. The most fun walking usually involves overcoming some kind of obstacle like wading across a river. In extreme rambling the idea is to seek out such obstacles. For example, river walking can be much enhanced by the purchase of a cheap pair of Chinese made chest waders (about £26). You can swim in these over the deep bits and wade through the rest — even in winter. Then when you arrive at the pub you can leave them outside and still be snug and dry.
¶ The Pillbox way. The OS coordinates of over 5,000 pillboxes in the UK are available in the book *Pillboxes* by Henry Wills. Henry Wills took fifteen years compiling this information as no record was kept of where pillboxes were being built. At one time (pre-internet) he financed his own pillbox hotline where people who found pillboxes could phone in the six figure coordinates. Henry Wills, now sadly dead, is one of the unwitting fathers of Extreme Rambling, as the pillbox information he collected reveals a series of lines across Britain every bit as compelling as more well known

'ways' like the Pennine way, South Downs Way etc etc. The main
pillbox way stretches from below Bristol all the way to Kent. To
walk this way you simply track along from pillbox to pillbox, rarely
looking inside as they are favoured by farmers and village teenagers
as places of dark mystery. Henry Wills book reveals the many and
varied designs of pillboxes, double ones, brick ones, even a few
disguised as shops, garages and bridges. I walked a wonderful
section of the pillbox way around the middle of Wiltshire, taking
in two white horses etched into the downs as a bonus.

¶ You can also make pillboxing competitive. As you don't know
exactly where they (they aren't marked on any map and coordinates
are only accurate to about 100m) there can be a prize for the first
person to spot one.

¶ The Didcot Power Walk. It is a piece of universal rural lore in the
Thames Valley that Didcot power station.

How to
MAKE YOUR OWN S&M TOYS
David Bramwell's guide for thrifty pervs

¶ Picture the scene: it's the end of the month, there's no money in the bank
and your partner is on his/her way round in an hour or two for that evening
of S&M you promised a week ago. And of course you've been so busy doing
nothing that you've forgotten to order online all those naughty toys. You
panic, fearing a punishment way beyond the boundaries of perverse sexual
pleasure! But worry not, below are some practical and easy solutions for
turning everyday household items into a whole range of S&M toys, thus
saving your ass. Or not, as the case may be...

¶ RUBBER WHIP: If you've got an old bike or bike wheel lying around,
take out the inner tube, clean it, cut out a section 80cm in length, splice one
end into nine strands each 50cm in length and you have a rather marvellous
and effective cat 'o' nine tails!

¶ PADDLE: An old table tennis bat is perfectly shaped for a spot of over-
the-knee correction. Simply strip off the rubber coating and steam off the
glue with a kettle. Hairbrushes, wooden spoons and spatulas will also do the
job almost as well.

¶ FLOGGER: Use an old leather belt.

¶ NIPPLE CLAMPS: Try clothes pegs. They might not look aesthetically
pleasing but are actually more adaptable than your standard nipple clamps
and can be hung on even more 'delicate' parts of the anatomy.

¶ COLLAR AND LESH: Pop down the local pet store and see what they've
got on offer; they're usually better and cheaper than the ones you find in sex
shops and the chains far sturdier. Plus there's something deliciously wrong

about shopping for sex toys when surrounded by guinea pigs, goldfish and puppies.

¶ HOT WAX PLAY: All you need is a few candles, a cigarette lighter and a dirty mind.

¶ MUMMIFICATION: Some folk like nothing better than being wrapped up like the remains of a Christmas turkey as part of their kinky bedroom game. You'll find the cling film in the kitchen drawer.

¶ CONDOMS: Why waste a fortune on prophylactics every time you have sex? Cat bladders make excellent condoms, and are strong, long-lasting and re-usable if washed. Simply coax a neighbour's cat that you don't like much into your house, strangle it, gut it, empty and wash the bladder and, hey presto, you've got a friend for life. And don't forget that catguts can even be used for stringing ukuleles! ☙

❖

Gardening
HOW TO GROW VEG WHEN YOU DON'T HAVE A GARDEN

Graham Burnett says that their land is your land

¶ Love the idea of growing your own fruit and vegetables but haven't got a garden of your own? Local allotments no longer exist or have full waiting lists? Don't despair, maybe guerrilla gardening is an option for you! Apply a little vision to the land around you; railway embankments, back gardens, golf courses, car parks, overgrown bits of land at your work-place and so on. Then give a little thought to clandestine cultivations — the only limits are those of your imagination. Herbs that thrive on poor soils could be grown amongst the thistles, rose-bay willow herb and buddlea on 'derelict' land earmarked for 'development'. Or a little known hole in a fence remembered from childhood explorations might provide opportunities for scrumping that long neglected orchard. And even if squatting empty property in your area is not an option (hello Neighbourhood Watch!) maybe the back gardens can still be put to use with a bit of cunning and stealth, or maybe seldom visited corners of local parks and gardens or even church yards? How about the flower beds that adorn your town centre if they're not too well looked after — you could be growing your crops right in the heart of the consumerist landscape of the burger bars, chain-stores and supermarkets — imagine the irony!
¶ Guerrilla gardening is also about ordinary people getting together to improve their environments and local communities without waiting for permission to do so. The movement has recently experienced an upsurge in interest due in no small part to the efforts of Richard Reynolds, host of www.guerrillagardening.org. He explains that "We do this because we cannot resist the satisfaction of turning a dilapidated patch of land into something more delightful. In place of compacted mud, rampant dandelions, and empty smoothie bottles we dig in manure, and plant hardy shrubs and luminous bedding." He also reminds us of George Orwell's observation about the

English: "All our culture that is most truly native centres round things which even when they are communal are not official." Indeed, many local authorities have been forced into a quandary by the unsanctioned improvement of neglected municipal eyesores. The green guerrillas who commit senseless acts of beauty by planting up roundabouts, verges and shopping centres from Stratford to Elephant and Castle are technically guilty of illegal trespass. But the spectacle of prosecutions would do little other than highlight officialdom's own lack of resources or commitment towards providing urban environments fit for the people they claim to serve.

¶ For my own part I'm proudest to have played a small role in creating Moon Corner on what used to be an unloved and littered spot beside a busy road in Leigh on Sea, Essex. Used for years as a dumping ground for shopping trolleys, old fridges and crisp packets, the site was cleared by local people to celebrate the anniversary of the post-war squatting movement and transformed into a beautiful micro-community garden. The Woodcraft Folk pruned and tidied the self-sewn sycamore and elders and planted bulbs and flowers, whilst a women's group created a locally distinctive mosaic using broken crockery. A bench was donated, and a mural painted on the wall with the message 'This is your space: please help to keep it tidy'. A decade later this tiny spot covering not more than a few square yards is still 'publicly owned' in the real sense of the word. Maybe not quite 'an urban adventure at the threshold of nature and culture' as the Situationist/radical guerrilla gardening Primal Seeds website would put it, but nonetheless a pleasant and relaxing green spot where harassed passers-by can rest and chat for a while without being bombarded by the 'product placement' messages that surround more and more of our 'designated high street seating areas'.

¶ In 1649 the original guerrilla gardener Gerard Winstanley observed that 'the earth is a common treasury for all', and anybody can literally sow their own small seeds without waiting for an official say-so. Not so long ago I found a handful of left over onion sets in my pocket when waiting for a train. I pushed these into the soil of a neglected border next to the bench, and hey presto, a few months later, free onions for anybody that cared to pick them! ⬡

Graham Burnett runs permaculture courses and is the author and illustrator of
Permaculture: a Beginners Guide and Earth Writings.
For more information see www.spiralseed.co.uk

William Yates

TEA: WHY DO LOVERS LEAP?

Chris Yates argues that a lack of good tea caused these sad deaths of yesteryear

¶ Throughout both recorded and mythical history lovers have been holding hands on some precipitous mountain ledge and then throwing themselves over the edge simply because they had been denied their wish to marry by a disapproving authority, usually parental. Sometimes, however, they leapt without arguing with anyone beacause either the girl was pregnant or one of them was already married to someone else. ¶ While this might seem a slightly extreme gesture of defiance in the face of unjust convention or an unsympathetic establishment, we must remember that most of the classic cases of leaping happened a long time ago, before the first pot of tea was smuggled out of China. It therefore seems fairly obvious to me that the lack of the magical brown leaf was the root cause of so much domestic disagree-ment and romantic disaster. Had the two sets of opposing parties been able to come together over a nice cup of tea their differences would have soon been resolved, and certain mountain ledges would have remained uncelebrated, except maybe for the view. ¶ This theory has a particular irony because one of the best teas in the world is called Lovers Leap, named after a legendary waterfall in the Sri Lankan mountains where the tea is grown. According to the legend, a King of long-ago decreed that his son, the Prince, must end his love affair with a beautiful girl because she was unworthy of him. Unable to countenance separation, the couple secretly met one last time, climbed to the high fall on the Pedro Mountain and married themselves to gravity. Centuries later, the nearby town of Nuwara Eliya became the home of the Pedro Tea Plantation, producing wonderful Ceylon teas that, had they been available during the reign of the King, would have ensured that everyone ended up living happily ever after. ¶ A few editions of the *Idler* ago, I described my first tasting of Lovers Leap, a single packet having been smuggled back for me from Sri Lanka. Such was my boundless delight, I said I would never be satisfied with any brew else and vowed to leave these shores and set up home next to the Pedro Mountain. But now it seems I can remain in Blighty after all. Lovers Leap is now available in the UK and the good people at Clipper Teas openly supply my needs and satisfy my craving — at £7.50 a packet. (Orders from 01308 8633440). However, if you make make that phone call and then discover that someone has just bought the entire stock, don't be too surprised. ◉

Angling

TIME TO MAKE THE
MOST OF IT

Wintertime: fish are hungry and the water is warm, says Kevin Parr

¶ The fish have been ravenous. ¶ With water temperatures both high and
constant, the standard winter slumber simply didn't happen last year. Some
anglers are delighted. The fish are easy to catch and also getting bigger and
bigger. ¶ I have been aware of noises being made along the lines of, 'Global
Warming?— bring it on!', and not with any hint of irony. ¶ It is unquestion-
able that climate change is affecting our rivers. ¶ Records are now not just
being broken but battered out of sight, and while improvements in fishing
technology and an ever increasing amount of fame hungry anglers chasing
known fish have played their part, the simple fact is that water temperatures
are on the rise. Fish, being cold-blooded, have little choice but to react with
it, eating more and becoming more active. ¶ Some cold water fish, such as
the Vendace and Arctic Char are facing extinction in Britain. The burbot has
already gone. ¶ And much as the warming sea is chasing the cod further
north and bringing Great Whites to our waters, so the great Scottish Lochs
will become weed-choked and silt ridden. Nessie will be left high and dry
amongst the water lilies. ¶ Not that Global Warming is a new fad. Climate
change has occurred since day dot, and will continue to do so for as long as
the sun burns. Indeed, Frost fairs on the Thames and pack-ice in the Hebrides
are not too distant events of history. ¶ And, while it is certainly not something
I will embrace, at least with my limited fishing time this season, I have been
able to catch a few fish. ¶ Not that the fish have been as important to me as in
the past, however. With moments more precious, I have appreciated every one
of them. I have seen the river like a dear old friend and enjoyed its company
as much as its contents. ¶ And the river has granted me a treat or two in
return, not least while I was giving a new rod a work-out. ¶ Through the
generosity of my late grandmother and also a dear friend, I now have in my
possession a split cane Avocet. I christened it with a roach and good company
but was ready to put a proper bend in it. ¶ The Kennet was eighteen inches

up and boiling, but I knew that if I could find a barbel then it wouldn't resist my garlic-spam, and with no-one else on the river I could travel light and have a good roam around. ¶ One spot was particularly inviting. A square yard of slack water had formed at the foot of a weir-sill and I found I could hold bottom with just a single swan-shot. With the rest of the weirpool heaving in a torrent of floodwater, there just had to be a fish there, but after a biteless half an hour I was on the move. ¶ I headed upstream, to spots which had produced me many a fish in the past, but my casts became half-hearted — nowhere had the same feel as the slack in the weirpool. ¶ After an inactive hour I had to head back to where I started, and I felt my confidence growing. I knew I was going to catch a barbel and I knew it was going to be a good one. ¶ I had never caught a fish from this spot, but the pieces were now in place — it was a simple matter of time. ¶ The bite was so lazy that for a second or two I was sure a branch had snagged my line, but then there was a kick and the fish eased out into the current. ¶ I applied sidestrain to keep the fish out of the main flow and a deadlock ensued that seemed to last a day before the barbel gradually began to cede line. ¶ I eased her into the steadier water beneath my feet and gave a heave to try and raise her in the water but she wouldn't budge — the rod was at full lock and I realised I would have to bide my time; something I'm not very good at.

¶ It isn't impatience on my part, but more an ever growing fear of losing the fish that has, in the past, prompted me to panic and ping the hook out. ¶ Here, however, I knew I had the right tool for the job. The Avocet was absorbing every thrust and head-shake with ease, and with a lovely fluid movement as well, unlike a carbon equivalent which tends to jerk around and test the hook-hold. ¶ My hook was holding firm, and as she rolled for the first time I knew I had a double-figure specimen. ¶ On the bank she looked even bigger, though the weight was all in the shoulders and belly. In fact, I had caught an eight-pounder a year to the week ago which was as long as this fish, so I was surprised to see the scales settle at thirteen pounds and six ounces. ¶ My second biggest barbel ever. ¶ And with the sun setting and a mist rising, a more perfect time to leave the company of an old friend couldn't have been wished for. ¶ If our climate really is going to change the world around us, then I, for one, will make the most of mother earth as I know her. ☙

In our consumer world, saturated by advertising and branded goods, is it possible to live without labels?

Neil Boorman decided to try. This is his story.

NEIL BOORMAN
BONFIRE OF THE BRANDS
HOW I LEARNT TO LIVE WITHOUT LABELS

ISBN: 978 1 84195 9870

www.canongate.net

£12.99

09.03.07 /
THE DAY I BURNT MY FAVOURITE TRAINERS

£12.99 Paperback
ISBN: 9781 84195 9870

UK Publication
6 September 2007

CANON GATE

BOOKSHELF

David Peace

Picture by Anna Pallai

7 REECE MEWS

FRANCIS BACON'S STUDIO

Darger

The Henry Darger C...
the American F...

HENRY

DARGER

ART AND SELECTED WRITINGS

MICHAEL BONESTEEL

William Blake

THE CO...

Francis Bacon:

THE ILLUSTRATED HISTO...

WALTER SIC...

BROMBERG

JHN
ARDS
RRY
DEN

BOOKS FOR KOOKS

James Bridle on why he is publishing dirty books

¶ Being a publisher these days is hard, with the supermarkets selling Richard & Judy picks, big corporations filling the shelves with any old crap they can get their hands on, and publishers in general afraid to get behind truly interesting and transgressive work. But it doesn't need to be this way. Technology really can do the work of a hundred men, leaving us to pick the forgotten and forbidden work that deserves an audience, and give it the platform it deserves.

¶ Bookkake is a new kind of publisher, one that uses new tech-nologies to drag publishing out of a corporate, Luddite torpor, but it's peddling a very old kind of book. In the tradition of such luminaries as Maurice Girodias and the Olympia Press, Bookkake is a publisher of dirty books.

¶ Whether it's Guillaume Apollinaire's Rakehell eavesdropping on the family servants confessing their unnatural encounters with geese to the local priest, or William Hazlitt breaking down in an career-destroying outburst of unrequited passion in his Liber Amoris, desire, love and sex have always created the most affecting and effective literature. But for too long much of such literature has been kept separate from the canon, like the room in the British Library reserved for readers of their 'specialist' collections of Victorian erotica, watched over by a bookish chaperone. Ironic, or course, as Apollinaire wrote The Amorous Exploits of a Young Rakehell, and several similar works, while employed at the Bibliothèque Nationale in Paris.

¶ The relationship between these two literatures has always been fluid and occasionally antagonistic. Stewart Home writes of Alexander Trocchi, whose literary career covered both fields, that 'Trocchi despised the bourgeois cultural order and in his porno-graphic works such as White Thighs he mocks it by using his mastery of literary technique for the ends of pastiche and parody. In this his pornographic works are quintessentially post modern, and move both beyond and behind the paradigmatically modernist concerns of his two 'serious' literary works *Young Adam* and *Cain's Book*.'

¶ Uncovering these works, and bringing them into the public consciousness, brings much of interest with it. Sean Walsh, in his introduction to *Fanny Hill*, reveals an ur-Fanny, not restrained within John Cleland's *Memoirs of a Woman of Pleasure*, but cavorting through the underbelly of the whole 18th Century. Her first appearance in the public record is in 1737, in the minutes of *The Order of the Beggar's Benison*, who met in Anstruther, Scotland, a full decade before the appearance of Cleland's novel:

> ¶ *1737. St. Andrew's Day. 24 met, 3 tested and enrolled. All frigged. The Dr. expatiated. Two nymphs, 18 and 19, exhibited as heretofore. Rules were submitted by Mr. Lumsdaine for future adoption. Fanny Hill was read. Tempest. Broke up at 3 o'clock a.m.*

¶ Walsh notes: 'The Beggar's Benison was, as the careful reader will have inferred, a sex club. It has a notable place in the the longish list of such societies in 18th-Century Britain; its unusually colourful prehistory of corrupt priests, early British Saints and folk fertility rites provides one distinction, while the happily full record we have of its arcana and rituals (the initiation ceremony, for example, seems to have consisted of the inductee's masturbating onto a large silver plate in front of the rest of the group) provides another.'

¶ Sex is also direct, and uncompromising: it breaks down the barriers between reader and author. In his 'Sadistic Introduction to a Masochistic Book', Leopold von Sacher-Masoch's *Venus In Furs*, the artist and writer Supervert highlights the sexuality of reading itself:

¶ 'In your mind there is only one posture for reading — a posture of submission. When you read you are always on your knees, humbly accepting your lessons from the writer god. Every reader is a zombie, a slave, a robot who wants to be programmed and controlled. You set aside your own thoughts for mine. Do it. Now.'

¶ There aren't enough dirty books around these days — and by dirty books we don't just mean grubby ones; we mean any books that get under your skin, that thicken the hair and collect under the fingernails; books that affect you physically, that move and change you. But sex — whether occurring in Cleland's riotous Covent Garden, or the imagined China of Octave Mirbeau's *The Torture Garden*, or Apollinaire's rural Château — is a good place to start. 🐌

Many of the books mentioned in this article are published by, or forthcoming, from Bookkake. For more information, visit www.bookkake.com.

KINKY BOOKS:
TOP TEN EROTICA

Mark Farley picks his all-time favourite erotic novels

¶ An utterly unique work, *The Story of O* by Pauline Reage is a land-mark novel of dominance and submission, a story of two people's intense love that influenced the many generations of sexually free spirits and open-minded deviants everywhere.

¶ *The Butcher* by Alina Reyes is a gradual and depraved exploration through torture and lust. A momentous novella about a young girl's summer job with a lecherous butcher who eventually relents him, her every desire.

¶ Helen Walsh's *Brass* is about a girl's friendship in Toxteth with a very violent old crush, revealed through self-destructive binges whilst she has powerful cravings for female prostitutes and strange men. Frank, coarse and graphic, it's Liverpool's *Trainspotting*.

¶ Once I finished Marthe Blau's *Submission*, I immediately lusted after another session with Elodie. The candour and graphic eroticism expel any myths about the alternative scene and leave you gagging to visit a contemporary Paris swingers club for yourself.

¶ Cult fifties classic *Beebo Brinker* by Anne Bannon fuelled the fire of the feminist movement. She wrote about equality, love and the unrequited lust and desire two women have for each other to a teasing, wonderful climax.

¶ Long before Catherine Millet, *The Ages of Lulu* by Almudena Grandes dazzled the literary world. Lulu's relationship with a much older man is an insatiable journey of new discoveries and power play, ending in a obscene and disturbing group scene.

¶ Tracy Quan's *Diary of a Married Call Girl* surpassed the first novel in content, maturity and eroticism. The aloofness and relaxed sexual confidence carries the sexy glamour and graphic encounters within and depict a juicy fantasy for multiple girl enthusiasts.

¶ With literary decadence, *The Torture Garden* by Octave Mirbeau is kinky. From the first page, it is a wonderful mesh of torture, pleasure and bliss. It envokes honesty, trust and sets the rules and benchmarks for alternative society.

¶ Anaïs Nin's *Little Birds* shouldn't be as beautiful and heart-warming as it is. It contains graphic images of worrying and circumspect topics but she writes with so much desire and agony, it's captivating. She was the foremost female diarist of her time also.

¶ Not just 'the bible of lesbianism', *The Well of Lonliness* by Radclyffe Hall is by rights a classic on transgenderism, politics and sex. Many called it obscene but it's a sign if anything that society has finally started to mature and grow up. Thank God.

❖

SEIZE THE MOMENT!

GWYN

GO ON!

THE PRETTY WOMEN OF PARIS

Irma de Bury
110B Boulevard Marlesherbes

¶ Another golden-haired beauty, of diminutive stature but well built, with a tip-tilted nose and a silvery laugh. She is young and always jolly. A fugitive from the bosom of her family at an early age, she ran away to Switzerland with a handsome soldier, who soon deserted her. Returning to Paris she appeared in the nocturnal haunts and was snapped up by a gentleman who spent his fortune with her. When the cupboard was bare, Irma, sooner than leave her protector, tried to work for her living and went out as a bonnet-builder. But the ruined gallant came into some money and abandoned the would-be milliner. So she stifled the aching of as kind a heart as ever beat behind a woman's left bubby, and fell into general circulation, where her modest bearing and tasty toilette soon caused her to reap a golden harvest. She has just appeared on the stage, where she was a doleful failure. At home she is sure of success, and is always ready for an encore. At supper she is invaluable as she laughs all night, cracks jokes incessantly, drinks her share of champagne, never gets drunk, and is always ready to retire behind a curtain, where her white hand and agile fingers will be found very efficacious for those who enjoy scientific masturbation.

extract from The Pretty Women of Paris (*Anonymous*)
illustrated by Lindsay Brunnock, limited edition hand-bound hardback, published by Hanbury Press, November 2007.
Handbury Press, The Gallery Workspace, Pennybank Chambers, 33–35 St John's Square, London EC1M 4DS

FIND YOUR VOICE

Idler lit ed Tony White on a new collection by John Berger

¶ In one of the essays collected here, 'Where Are We?', the indefatigable writer, artist and above all Humanist, John Berger speculates about George W Bush and his cohorts' rise to power ('How did [they] get where they did?'), then rejects the question as too rhetorical. Flipping it, he realises that, instead, we need to engage with the pain that they and other fanatics have caused.
¶ It's always a pleasure to read John Berger — he casts his net wide. Indeed, reflecting on the pitilessness and universality of the painter Francis Bacon's vision (a universality nourished, he says, merely by 'the melodramas of a very provincial bohemian circle'), Berger has a further insight: to engage with the vocabulary of those in power, 'only adds to the surrounding murkiness and devastation'. The revelation that follows — and which we can share — is that the appropriate response to this is not silence: 'It means choosing the voices one wishes to join.'
¶ Berger's sympathy is clearly with those who have been *denied* a voice. Whether he's writing of young Palestinians attempting to grow crops beneath the gaze of a hostile military, or of those people travelling to work who were caught in the London bombings of 7 July 2005; those 'vulnerable people, struggling to survive and make some sense of their lives'.
¶ Berger's generosity in all this, his apparent desire to use the best of his efforts to engage with and elucidate seemingly intractable problems, *and* to communicate these processes in terms that most readers might understand, is inspirational. It also engenders a succinctness that is as simply refreshing as a glass of water in face of Bush, Blair and co's 'interminably repetitive speeches, announcements, press conferences and threats': 'We have to reject the new tyranny's discourse. Its terms are crap.' ☺

John Berger, Hold Everything Dear, Verso, £12.99

DON'T X-CERT YOURSELF

Our man in the back row with the overpriced chocolate
raisins and a tissue on his thigh: Paul Hamilton.

¶ 'Pornography is the theory,' my dear old radical feminist art
teacher would postulate,' and RAPE IS THE ACT!!!'

¶ Why the joyless old bat would scream this mantra whilst me and
the other pimply students were painting ghastly daubs of a 70 year
old male model was never clear. For one thing, it never made much
sense to me: the porn enthusiast, after a close study of his grumble
vid to inspire him to take the top off his egg, wouldn't have the
energy to go haring into the streets and raping some passer-by.
However, she did have a point in that women were sexually
exploited in films (and any other medium) — but who is
responsible for the exploiting? A quick glance at the millions
of porn websites will show countless women filmed and
photographed in sexual congress. Who is exploiting whom?
Are we to believe that all these women are forced against their will
at gunpoint or by pointy sticks to indulge in these acts? Are there
no women who like fucks for fuck's sake, like money, thrill-seeking,
exhibiting themselves? Are they traitors to feminism? Even some of
the staunchest of feminists have admitted having rape fantasies —
ever notice how the audience goes quiet when Diane Keaton in *Play
It Again, Sam* (1972) admits to Woody Allen that she might enjoy the
experience? (Ah, but Allen wrote that dialogue: is he using Keaton
to express his own secret desire?) If one was to pinpoint the actual
exact moment where feminism was abandoned as a force for
societal change and conscience-revelation — and, let's face it, we
are in the movement-abandoning split-second-identification trade
here — it could very well be in the closing minutes of *Grease* (1978)
as prim student Olivia Newton-John surrenders to gum-chewin'

The Night Porter (1974)

peer pressure and trades in her specs and schoolbooks to become a
leather-trousered slut, another piece of meat for the quiffabillies to
fight over or pass around.

¶ The problem is, of course, that the true sensations are happening
inside the bodies of screwer and screwee, and these elated passions
cannot be adequately, let alone poetically, expressed as pure shared
sensual pleasure to the onlooker. Allied to this is the matter of role-
play and where the mind goes. A delightful example of role-play
taken to its zenith by Dirk Bogarde and Charlotte Rampling in
The Night Porter (1974). Dirk is a former Nazi officer stationed at a
concentration camp during the war, now living a quiet peacetime
existence in a Viennese hotel. His tedious routine is broken by the
appearance of furs-and-jewels-bedecked Charlotte. They recognise
each other immediately: she was regularly raped by him at the
camp. With her orchestra-conducting husband out of the frame,
they re-enact their sadomasochistic relationship. Their chance
encounter has brought their dull, orderly, predictable present in
sharp contrast with the life-and-death intensity of their past. She
knows that, by subjecting her to torture and sexual domination,

The Story Of O *(1975)*

he saved her from the gas chamber. Removed from his position
of power, and feeling guilt-ridden by the liberties he took and
violated, the master/slave axis eventually favours her. *The Night Porter*,
as an allegory of fascism and humanity's obsessive desire for
degradation, is no profound meditation. It is unsettling (especially
the scenes of Rampling as the victimised girl) but also rather
boring. A bit like sex itself, sometimes.

¶ When Anne Desclos' publisher husband pontificated that women
were incapable of producing erotica, she rose to the challenge bril-
liantly. *Histoire d'O*, printed under the pseudonym Pauline Reage, was
a mid-1950s sensation, with its salacious tales of a college whereby
willing women enrol to become sex slaves. The 1975 film adapta-
tion, *The Story Of O*, is faithful to the original fantasy — and Corinne
Clery is occasionally unintentionally hilarious in the title role (it's a
tricky path to negotiate, the necessary suspension of disbelief
giving way to ludicrous po-facedness), but who could fail to be
ridiculous when they agree to unreservedly be the sex slave to men
with flares like giant shark fins? The problem with O is the dreamy,
slo-mo direction by the ludicrously-named Just Jaeckin. No matter

how savage the whippings and genital brandings get, you tend to feel you're floating through a 90-minute Flake commercial. The underlying feminist ideology that women prove themselves stronger and more worthy than men by suffering physical and mental indignities in the name of love is tokenist pants, of course.

¶ There has been enough written about Russ Meyer, the tiresome tit fetishist, and his obsessions (women with chests like a dead heat in a zeppelin race cavorting with rednecks with five foot long wankwands or Adolf Hitler and his chums), so let's discuss his European brother-in-lust, Tinto Brass, an indefatigable bum worshipper whose jumbled mess of deviant obsession and sexism tends to be passed off as lovable eccentric free-love philosophy. 'You cannot believe a woman by studying her face,' he expounds: 'You must learn to read a woman's arse. It never lies.' (What are you babbling about, Tints? A woman's arse is like you — full of shit.) Despite his predilection, Brass The Arse has proved himself capable of producing some thoughtful and entertaining films: *Black Angel* (2000), set in the last days of World War II, has wealthy Italian milf Anna Galiena losing her heart (and fascist dosh) in an adulterous affair with an irresistible hunk of blond Nazi beefcake Gabriel Garko. They all die in the end, so that's all right then. Amongst the sumptuous set dressings and obligatory orgy scene (threaded through by a conga-line of grinning twits led by a Gestapo-jacketed babe thrusting a three-foot gold-painted phallus), there's a woman-sniffing-cocaine moment which triggers the compulsory seeing-through-drugged-up-eyes effect that only serves to alert every viewer that this man has no idea what drugs are. *Cheeky* (2000) finds Brass at his investigative, campaigning best: were it not for this film I'd have been eternally ignorant of the whole blue-wigged lesbian estate agent orgy fandango that holds London in its long-gloved grip.

¶ Brass's outlook is pretty harmless, really — conventional even. Spinal Tap's Mendocino rocket-fuel-glugging keyboardist Viv Savage's maxim 'Have a good time all the time' pretty much encapsulates Brass's worldview. If you're young and beautiful then what could be more fun than taking your clothes off and fucking — apart from having someone old and ugly behind the camera capturing it all, of course? He is essentially an innocent — like Benny Hill, he practices the art of Phwooarghnography — and seems blithely, or balefully, ignorant of the darker sexual impulses and exploitative nature of Man. (Annabel Chong is similar in this regard. A gender studies student in America, she decides to star in a hardcore humpathon, fucking and sucking 251 men in one ten hour session, as a display of her feminist principles and that it is she who is the exploiter rather than the exploited. It doesn't turn out that way, as the documentary *Sex:The Annabel Chong Story* [1999] predictably and heartbreakingly shows.)

¶ Brass found himself utterly out of his depth directing Penthouse publisher Bob Guccionne's production of *Caligula* which was filmed in 1976 but finally released three years later after much meddling and reshooting by Guccionne himself. Brass seemed to have wanted to recreate the debauched and sated sensuality of *Fellini's Satyricon* (1969) but Guccionne demanded a level of depravity to which the director could not descend. Hacked to the brim of incomprehensibility, the DVD remains, in *Time Out* magazine's classic two-word review, 'Fucking weary' and one can only wonder what was in the minds of the distinguished thesps — Gielgud, O'Toole, Mirren, Malcolm McDowell (all British, of course; it's that old Hollywood tradition of all Roman Empire nasties having English accents) — whilst they swanned around in togas and laurels. Perhaps it's the same thought that may have persuaded the cream of British acting and comedy talent — John LeMesurier, Irene Handl, Harry H. Corbett ('The British Brando' of the 1950s theatre!), et al — to appear in that miserable, oxymoronic, poxy, moronic genre, the sex comedy; namely, it's a nice wad of cash for a film that'll be on the screens for three weeks tops, whereupon it'll disappear forever, become totally forgotten, my reputation intact. How were they to know that home video was waiting in the wings, hand-in-hand with the trash aesthetic?

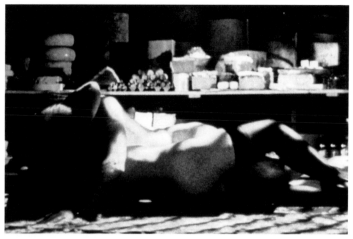

The Cook, The Thief, His Wife And Her Lover (1989)

¶ *Caligula* is repugnance personified. Apart from a brief moment when Helen Mirren comforts the maniac emperor (McDowell), the film is bereft of tenderness, compassion, care, love. In one horrible scene, Caligula wrecks a wedding service by raping the bride and then finger-fucking the groom's anus. It's humanity at its basest, on that sublevel with Pasolini's rotten-to-its-cold-heart *Salo* (1975). Cold, manipulative, hateful — this is Scornography. Shamefully, I admit there is something deeply arousing when McDowell leads Mirren through a banquet with a leash attached to a collar round her throat — ah, but call me old-fashioned.

¶ Mirren had to contend with another megalomaniac sadist, this time more successfully, in *The Cook, The Thief, His Wife And Her Lover* (1989), as the humiliated, eternally-suffering wife of a moneyed über-yob, played with almost hammy relish by Michael Gambon. Regular diners at punishing glutton Gambon's own restaurant, Mirren steals away from him, his cronies and his endless game of tirades for relief in the form of lavatory love with an anonymous man. The sex they share is exciting — daring, caring, yet uncaring — and it moves us, the viewer, because we know she hasn't been touched so tenderly, so longingly, for so long. So much sex in films

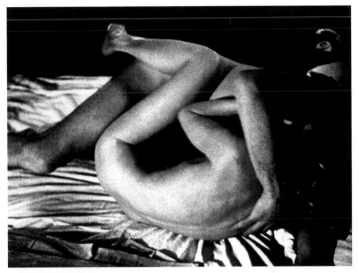

Don't Look Now (1973)

is of this furtive, adulterous nature, though: don't any *husbands and wives* do it, and be *happy* doing it?

¶ Julie Christie and Donald Sutherland play a couple some five years into their marriage in *Don't Look Now* (1973). The power and life-affirming joy in their lovemaking scene ('sex scene' is crass here) works on various levels. The occasion occurs a few weeks following the death by drowning of their little girl, and, more than lust, their passionate dance is a bonding of their happiness of what was, their sorrow and mourning of what is, and their determination and commitment to remain together for whatever may be. Director Nic Roeg underlines the implicit restating of the wedding vows, 'in sickness and in health, till death us do part', by intercutting the love scene with Sutherland and Christie, post-coitus, getting dressed for dinner.

¶ Roeg, in his time-fascinated films, never separates sex from the rest of life. The beginning of *Performance* (1970) flicks back and forth between rough sex (gangster James Fox and his girlfriend indulging in mock-violence, bondage and a blowjob whilst he

Don't Look Now (1973)

admires himself in a hand mirror) and a Rolls Royce travelling a
pre-rush hour motorway: this is the car he will later pour sulphuric
acid over and whose chauffeur he will torture. *Bad Timing* (1980)
combines footage of Theresa Russell at the height of sexual ecstasy
with a shots of her having her stomach pumped by medics after her
suicide bid; almost literally coming and going at the same time. If
only more directors were as imaginative as Roeg. Stanley Kubrick
was a sexual dunderhead, women being mainly decoration and
furniture in his peripheral vision. In his second, zero budget,
feature, *Killer's Kiss* (1955), however, there is an erotic charge in the
shoot-out held in a warehouse full of female showroom dummies.
Kubrick, sadly, never developed this kinky side, although his wife
Christiane provided some of the exuberantly sexual paintings in *A
Clockwork Orange* (1971). Kubrick's direction of ... *Orange* borders on
the voyeuristic: See when the naked woman runs from the theatre
stage, away from Billy Boy and his merry gang of rapists, the
camera follows her progress, Kubrick lasciviously lapping up every

swing of the poor woman's breasts. His decision to increase *Lolita's* age from 12 to 15 is regrettable if not cowardly (it was in pre-production whilst the *Lady Chatterley's Lover* court case was in session), but the sexual aesthetic of *Eyes Wide Shut* (1999) betrays a stifling conservatism, a dullard's morality. It begins so well, with Nicole Kidman wiping her wizard's beard following a piss — a wonderfully natural human moment (and it only required 759 takes) — but the opportunities for exploring and extending the cinematic potential of erotica were sadly undisturbed. The masked orgy sequence was as tame and lame as anything devised by that celebrated pipe-sucking emotional retard Hugh Hefner, and Kubrick's lack of foresight in employing Nicole Kidman to play a multitude of temptresses for Tom Cruise to encounter is disastrous. This Kubrick's Pube is a lamentable swansong, not worth a wank.

¶ A brilliantly-conceived and executed speculation on the effects of an increasingly automated technocracy on love and sex is David Cronenberg's 1996 *Crash*. Bored, jaded, spoilt middle-class straights get their kicks watching videos of, and enacting, car crashes. Black plastic-clad Rosanna Arquette has a gaping wound in her thigh (sustained from an auto-wrecking) used as a surrogate vagina by James Spader. At the finish of the film, Spader drives Deborah Kara Unger's car off the road, pulls her out and fucks her. Unger weeps, not in shock or pain, but because she realises she will survive. Her wish is to die at the moment of orgasm. The crash victims' twisted limbs are sublime metaphors for the way humanity must bend itself to accommodate a world increasingly controlled by computers and cybernetics. Techno prisoners indeed.

¶ Recent sexual developments in mainstream cinema have seen authentic genital penetration, as well as fellatio and cunnilingus action. Oh, hoo-chuffing-ray. From the 1896 silent short *The May Irwin And John C. Rice Kiss* (it's exactly what it says on the box) to the see-you-later-ejaculator of *9 Songs* one hundred and eight years later, it's been a long time coming.

¶ Anyone up for pizza?

WHATEVER YOU DO,
TAKE PRIDE.

Further Viewing

Bedazzled (1967) — 'Fornication's such a puny sin.'

Harold And Maude (1972)

Behind Convent Walls (1977)

Baise-Moi (2000)

In The Realm Of The Senses (Ai No Corrida) (1976)

Betty Blue (1986)

A Bigger Splash (1975)

Alfie (1966)

Porky's (1981)

Morocco (1930) — drag king Marlene Dietrich kisses another
woman.

The System (1964) — Oliver Reed is the first person to say 'fuck'
onscreen, the devil! (Speaking of which ...)

The Devils (1971)

Cruising (1980)

Secretary (2002)

Demon Seed (1977)

Nine And A Half Weeks (1986) — and they called it Yuppy Love.

Love Is The Devil (1998)

Belle De Jour (1967)

The Servant (1963)

The Rocky Horror Picture Show (1975)

La Dolce Vita (1960)

The Adventures Of A Private Eye (1977) — maybe the worst of the dire
Seventies British Sex Comedies, certainly the one most lacking
in humanity: the last scene has ex-Dr Who Jon Pertwee, hair like
a gigantic scoop of ice cream, reclining naked in his office.
Somebody knocks an electric fan off a cabinet. It lands in his
lap, castrating him instantly. The assorted witnesses give rueful
smiles and the soundtrack issues a 'wah-wah-waaaaaaaaah' on
a trumpet. 🐌

14 YEARS of IDLENESS

& *the occasional publication . . .*

1: August '93
SOLD OUT
Dr Johnson
Terence McKenna

2: Nov–Dec '93
SOLD OUT
Homer Simpson
Will Self

3: Jan–Feb '94
£8.00
Bertrand Russell
Charles Handy

4: April–May '94
SOLD OUT
Kurt Cobain
Matt Black

5: July–Aug '94
SOLD OUT
Douglas Coupland
Jerome K Jerome

6: Sept–Oct '94
SOLD OUT
Easy Listening
Richard Linklater

7: Dec–Jan '95
SOLD OUT
Sleep
Gilbert Shelton

8: Feb–Mar '95
SOLD OUT
Jeffrey Bernard
Robert Newman

9: May–June '95
SOLD OUT
Suzanne Moore
Positive Drinking

10: July–Aug '95
SOLD OUT
Damien Hirst
Will Self

11: Sept–Oct '95
£4.00
Keith Allen
Dole Life

12: Nov–Dec '95
£4.00
Bruce Robinson
All Night Garages

TO ORDER YOUR BACK ISSUES:
Go to www.idler.co.uk, or call 020 7691 0320 with your credit card, or make a cheque out to 'The Idler' and send it to: The Idler, Studio 20, 24–28A Hatton Wall, London EC1N 8JH. You must include P&P cost as follows:
Issues 1–24: 50p per issue. Issues 25–34: £2 per issue.
T-shirts £1 per item.
For European Community, add 50%. For Rest of the World, add 100%

39
BACK
ISSUES

13: Jan–Feb '96	14: Mar–Apr '96	15: May–Jun '96	16: Aug–Sept '96
SOLD OUT	**£4.00**	**SOLD OUT**	**SOLD OUT**
Stan Lee	Bruce Reynolds	Hashish Killers	John Michel
Life As A Kid	Will Self	Alex Chilton	World Poker

17: Nov–Dec '96	18: Spring '97	19: Summer '97	20: Winter '97
SOLD OUT	**SOLD OUT**	**£4.00**	**SOLD OUT**
John Cooper Clarke	Thomas Pynchon	Psychogeography	Howard Marks
Cary Grant	Ivan Illich	Henry Miller	Kenny Kramer

21: Feb–March '98	22: April–May '98	23: June–July '98	24: Aug–Sep '98
SOLD OUT	**SOLD OUT**	**SOLD OUT**	**SOLD OUT**
The Gambler	Alan Moore	Summer Special	Krazy Golf
Bez	Alex James	Tim Roth	David Soul

MAN'S RUIN
25: Winter 1999
£15
The first book-format Idler, featuring Louis Theroux's Sick Notes, Will Self, Howard Marks, Adam and Joe and Ken Kesey

PARADISE
26: Summer 2000
£5
Jonathan Coe meets David Nobbs, Nicholas Blincoe on Sherlock Holmes, Tiki Special, Iain Sinclair on the London Eye

THE FOOL
27: Winter 2000
£5
Village Idiots, Arthur Smith's diary, The Big Quit, James Jarvis's World Of Pain, John Lloyd

RETREAT
28: Summer 2001
£10
Louis Theroux meets Bill Oddie, Jonathan Ross meets Alan Moore, Alex James meets Patrick Moore, plus Andrew Loog Oldham

HELL
29: Winter 2001
£10
Crass founder Penny Rimbaud, Crap Jobs Special, Boredom Section, New fiction from Niall Griffiths, Mark Manning, Billy Childish

LOVE
30: Summer 2002
£10
Louis Theroux meets Colin Wilson, Johnny Ball on Descartes, Crap Towns, Devon Retreat, Chris Yates interview, Marchesa Casati

REVOLUTION
31: Winter 2002
£10
Dave Stewart, Black Panthers, Saint Monday, Allotments, Riots, Introducing the Practical Idler section

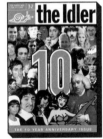

ANNIVERSARY
32: Winter 2003
£10
Damien Hirst on why cunts sell shit to fools, Marc Bolan, the pleasures of the top deck, Walt Whitman, happiness

To order go to
www.idler.co.uk

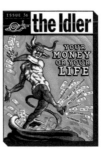

LADIES OF LEISURE
33: Spring 2004
£10
Clare Pollard is sick of shopping, Girls on bass, the wit and wisdom of Quentin Crisp; Barbara Ehrenreich

THE FOOD ISSUE
34: Winter 2004
£10
Joan Bakewell on life as a freelancer, Bill Drummond's soup adventure, The Giro Playboy, Falconry, why supermarkets are evil and Jerome K Jerome

WAR ON WORK
35: Spring 2005
£10
Keith Allen's A to Z of life, Raoul Vaneigem interview, Jeremy Deller's Folk Art, Dan Kieran's Seven Steps To The Idle Life, Chris Donald, Peter Doherty and more Crap Jobs

YOUR MONEY OR YOUR LIFE
36: Winter 2005
£10
Mutoid Waste Company, Edward Chancellor on credit, Penny Rimbaud, Jay Griffiths, A Hitch Hiker's Guide, the Guilds, Chris Donald

CHILDISH THINGS
37: Spring 2005
£10
Childcare for the Lazy, Michael Palin, Bertrand Russell, Free Range Education, Running Away to Join the Circus

THE GREEN MAN
38: Winter 2006
£10.99
Stephen Harding on why doing less is the way forward, Richard Benson tries to sow a meadow, in conversation with Jamie Reid, John Michell on Cobbett, plus ukulele special

LIE BACK & PROTEST
39: Spring 2007
£10.99
Penny Rimbaud on The Meaning of Life, Jay Griffiths eats missionaries for breakfast, Ronald Hutton, Green Gartside, LA Rowland explains why we shouldn't bother going to university

To order go to
www.idler.co.uk